Journey with us.
www.yonderpublishing.com

Published in 2016 by Yonder Publishing, UK.

Designed and Produced by Natalie Fox.

ISBN: 978-0-9935382-2-3

Affirmations Journal For Self-Love and Confidence.
Using Gratitude and The Law Of Attraction To Change
The Way You Feel About Yourself.

Available from Amazon.com and other retail outlets.

www.natalielouisefox.com

www.yonderpublishing.com
hello@yonderpublishing.com

Affirmations Journal

For Self-Love and Confidence

USING GRATITUDE AND THE LAW OF ATTRACTION TO CHANGE THE WAY YOU FEEL ABOUT YOURSELF

Natalie L Fox

Introduction

Some of you may have used affirmations before with hit-or-miss results. Some of you may never have heard of affirmations before. This book will help you to master them!

So what exactly is an affirmation?

It's basically a way of installing a new subconscious belief into your mind. Affirmations can be a powerful catalyst for change if you use them correctly.

The way we view ourselves in the world very often comes from deep emotional programming that we received as a child. This may be because of your parents, friends or an authority figure such as a particular teacher. For example, if you felt like you were inadequate in any way because of something that you did (that your parents didn't think may have been good enough), this will really affect your confidence as an adult. Perhaps you weren't allowed things but your siblings were; this will make you feel like you are unworthy for whatever reason. Perhaps you were good at some things but not others and you were penalised for this. Perhaps you just didn't receive any attention as a child or you were told that you were 'naughty'.

These messages, repeated over time may install the belief that you are not good enough, or that you don't deserve to be loved. As an adult, you may have been treated badly in a relationship and you may have formed the subconscious belief that you are unlovable.

Loving yourself is really important for your personal and spiritual growth and if you don't love yourself, then this is something that you need to overcome. Not in an arrogant way, but in a way that means you are kind, patient and caring towards yourself. If you can feel real love for yourself your confidence levels will soar, and so will your success.

Affirmations are statements set in the present tense, in a positive manner. A good example of an affirmation would be: "I am enough". Repetition of these positive statements will mean that they sink into your subconscious mind and after time and you will start to run on this new programming by default. This opens the door to a new level of respect for yourself and you will be able to move away from self-defeating and destructive behaviours.
There are two caveats to this though.

1. The affirmations will only work if they do not conflict with an existing belief. If you have a conflicting belief such as "I'm useless at everything", then the affirmation "I feel good about myself" will feel like a lie. This book will help you to uncover those hidden beliefs deep in your subconscious so that you can get to work on correcting them (you can do this as you go along as you will likely find affirmations that feel more untrue than others. There is also a special section at the back of this book to journal about those hidden beliefs and start to release them).

2. You have to commit to repetition. Children learn faster than adults, that is a documented fact. To add to this, many beliefs may have formed during childhood which carry an intense emotional charge. To neutralise this, as an adult, you have to repeat the affirmations over and over, just like when you had to learn your times tables at school! Use this book to start the process and then commit your affirmation to memory to use silently in your head for the whole day. You can repeat the affirmation whilst washing up, waiting for a bus, standing in a queue, driving your car. Do it whenever and wherever you can, but make sure it is often.

My take on affirmations is that by adding gratitude to them, you accelerate the results. As I mentioned before, some beliefs are wedged in our minds due to an intense emotional charge. For example, imagine the negative emotional charge you would feel if you found out a partner was cheating on you. You may form a belief that ALL partners can't be trusted, and develop a fear of it happening again. This is of course, untrue, as not every potential partner would be like that, however, you may (via the Law Of Attraction) attract more partners with unfaithful tendencies until you clear it.

Gratitude carries a really, really positive emotional charge. So when you are affirming, you can attach this positive emotional charge to your words. This really super-charges your affirmations and makes the process of installing these new beliefs much, much quicker. Gratitude is magical and practicing it can bring the most profound results in all areas of your life, as I have seen with myself and the purchasers of my first book, Gratitude Journal: 100 Days Of Gratitude Will Change Your Life.
If you want to take the practice of gratitude further or find out more about the Law Of Attraction, I encourage you to check out my website **www.natalielouisefox.com** where you will find lots of helpful information.

This book has four sections. The first section is where you will practice your affirmations for 100 days. Each day a different affirmation is set for you. You need to say the affirmation out loud with your hand on your heart. You can also tap the top of your head at the crown chakra point too whilst saying it if you don't mind looking a little bit silly - it works!

Once you have stated the affirmation, you write it out ten times and then finish by putting your hand on your heart and making a declaration of gratitude. Then for the rest of the day, silently repeat the affirmation AS MUCH AS YOU CAN. If you can say it out loud without getting funny looks, that's ok too. Whenever a negative thought 'pops' into your head, simply observe it and then say your affirmation to cancel it. Try to think of more things to be grateful for too as you go throughout your day, as this will raise your energy up higher.

The second section allows you to journal about any limiting beliefs that you may discover along the way. There are some helpful suggestions to clear these beliefs. For some people, other mind-body tools may be helpful too, such as energy clearing, hypnosis or Emotional Freedom Technique (EFT).

The third section provides space to write any of your own affirmations down that you may wish to enter into the mix. Don't ignore these, sometimes they are the ones you need to work on first.

The final section is for 'Little Love Moments' and allows you to document evidence that your affirmations are working. Don't forget to use this bit! It's fun and can provide you with the proof you need to create bigger and better things!

Good luck and I hope that you enjoy using this book. If you have any inspiring stories about your journey we'd love to hear them. Please send them to hello@yonderpublishing.com

You can find out more about me, my work and my other books by heading over to **www.natalielouisefox.com**

Love and blessings,

Natalie x

1. Change your conscious thoughts.

2. Change your subconscious thoughts.

3. Raise your energy up with gratitude.

DESCRIBE HOW YOU CURRENTLY FEEL ABOUT YOURSELF IN DETAIL. TALK ABOUT YOUR EXPERIENCES, FEARS, PROBLEMS AND BLOCKS:

....

....

....

....

....

....

....

....

....

....

....

....

....

....

....

....

DESCRIBE HOW CONFIDENT AND LOVING YOU WANT TO FEEL. TALK ABOUT YOUR HOPES, DREAMS AND HOW YOU WANT TO CHANGE:

....

....

....

....

....

....

....

....

....

....

....

....

....

....

....

....

LET'S START!

Right Now, I'm Grateful for These 3 Things:

___

___

___

Post your starting list on our Facebook wall!
www.facebook.com/gratitudejournal

Day 1

SAY THIS AFFIRMATION OUT LOUD WITH YOUR HAND ON YOUR HEART:

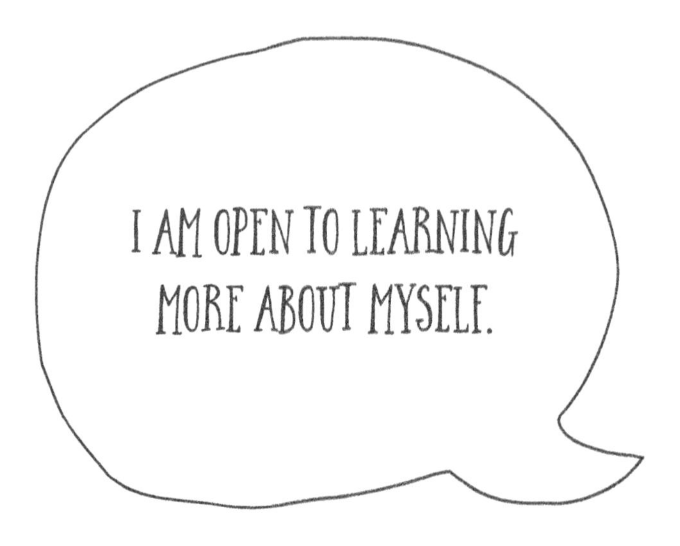

NOW WRITE IT OUT 10 TIMES:

1 ....

....

2 ....

....

3 ....

....

4 ....

....

5 ....

....

6 ....

....

7 ....

....

8 ....

....

9 ....

....

10 ....

....

NOW REPEAT THIS THREE TIMES WITH YOUR HAND ON YOUR HEART:

♥♥♥

"I LOVE LEARNING MORE ABOUT MYSELF AND I APPRECIATE EVERYTHING I LEARN."

♥♥♥

NOW WRITE HOW YOU FEEL AFTER COMPLETING THIS EXCERCISE. DOES IT BRING ANYTHING UP FOR YOU? HOW DO YOU WANT TO FEEL TODAY?

....

....

....

SAY THIS AFFIRMATION OUT LOUD WITH YOUR HAND ON YOUR HEART:

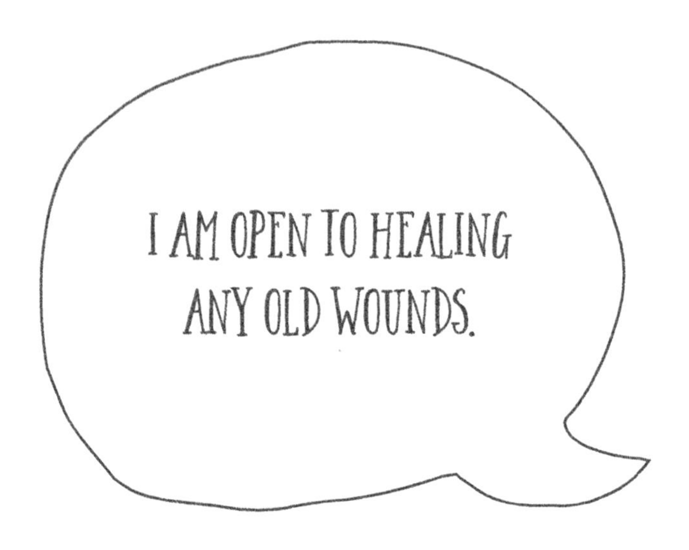

NOW WRITE IT OUT 10 TIMES:

1 ....

....

2 ....

....

3 ....

....

4 ....

....

5 ....

....

6 ....

....

7 ....

....

8 ....

....

9 ....

....

10 ....

....

NOW REPEAT THIS THREE TIMES WITH YOUR HAND ON YOUR HEART:

♥♥♥

"I'M SO HAPPY AND GRATEFUL THAT IT'S POSSIBLE TO HEAL OLD WOUNDS FOR GOOD."

♥♥♥

NOW WRITE HOW YOU FEEL AFTER COMPLETING THIS EXCERCISE. DOES IT BRING ANYTHING UP FOR YOU? HOW DO YOU WANT TO FEEL TODAY?

....

....

....

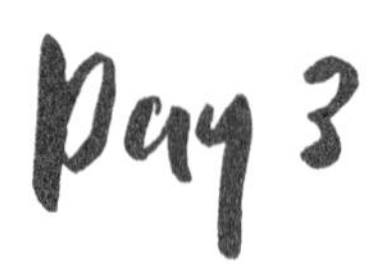

SAY THIS AFFIRMATION OUT LOUD WITH YOUR HAND ON YOUR HEART:

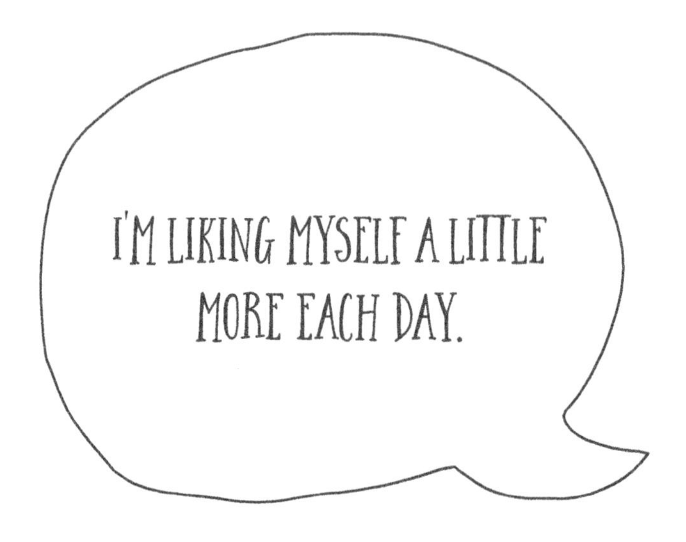

NOW WRITE IT OUT 10 TIMES:

1 ....

....

2 ....

....

3 ....

....

4 ....

....

5 ....

....

6 ....

....

7 ....

....

8 ....

....

9 ....

....

10 ....

....

NOW REPEAT THIS THREE TIMES WITH YOUR HAND ON YOUR HEART:

♥♥♥

"I REALLY LOVE AND APPRECIATE THE FACT THAT I'M LIKING MYSELF A LITTLE MORE EACH DAY."

♥♥♥

NOW WRITE HOW YOU FEEL AFTER COMPLETING THIS EXCERCISE. DOES IT BRING ANYTHING UP FOR YOU? HOW DO YOU WANT TO FEEL TODAY?

....

....

....

SAY THIS AFFIRMATION OUT LOUD WITH YOUR HAND ON YOUR HEART:

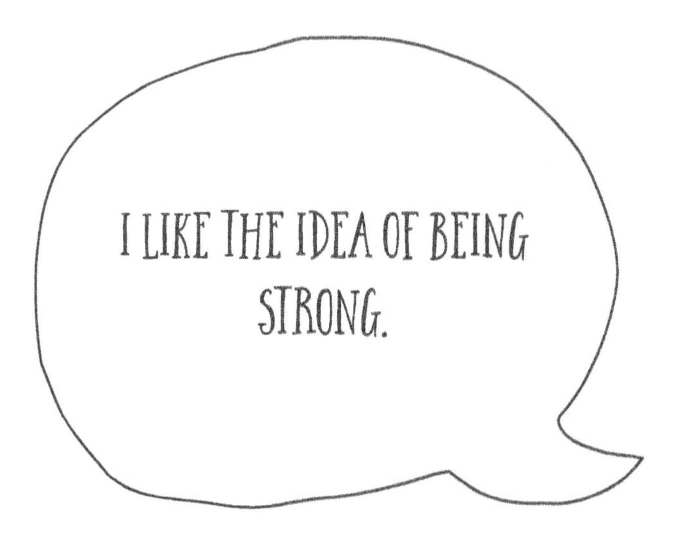

NOW WRITE IT OUT 10 TIMES:

1 ....

....

2 ....

....

3 ....

....

4 ....

....

5 ....

....

6 ....

....

7 ....

....

8 ....

....

9 ....

....

10 ....

....

NOW REPEAT THIS THREE TIMES WITH YOUR HAND ON YOUR HEART:

♥♥♥

"I LOVE THE IDEA OF HARNESSING MY INNER-STRENGTH."

♥♥♥

NOW WRITE HOW YOU FEEL AFTER COMPLETING THIS EXCERCISE. DOES IT BRING ANYTHING UP FOR YOU? HOW DO YOU WANT TO FEEL TODAY?

....

....

....

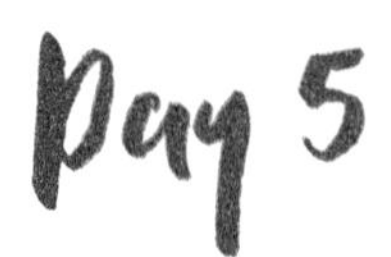

Day 5

SAY THIS AFFIRMATION OUT LOUD WITH YOUR HAND ON YOUR HEART:

NOW WRITE IT OUT 10 TIMES:

1 ....

....

2 ....

....

3 ....

....

4 ....

....

5 ....

....

6 ....

....

7 ....

....

8 ....

....

9 ....

....

10 ....

....

NOW REPEAT THIS THREE TIMES WITH YOUR HAND ON YOUR HEART:

♥♥♥

"I'M SO HAPPY AND GRATEFUL FOR EVERY PART OF MY BODY. IT IS TRULY AMAZING."

♥♥♥

NOW WRITE HOW YOU FEEL AFTER COMPLETING THIS EXCERCISE. DOES IT BRING ANYTHING UP FOR YOU? HOW DO YOU WANT TO FEEL TODAY?

....

....

....

Day 6

SAY THIS AFFIRMATION OUT LOUD WITH YOUR HAND ON YOUR HEART:

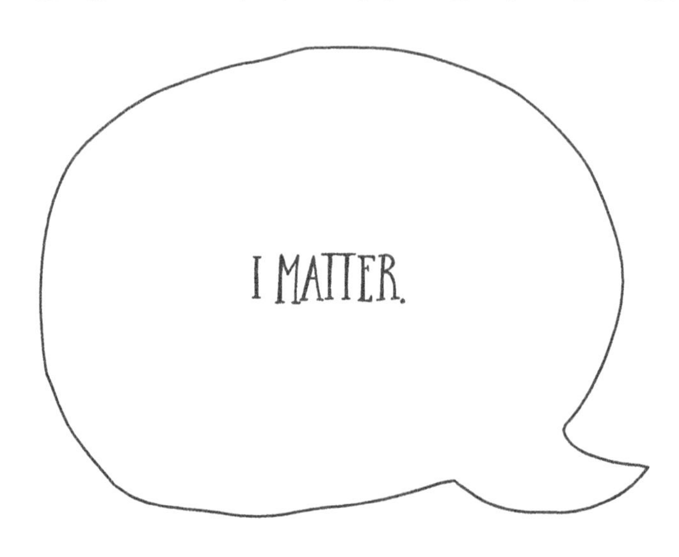

NOW WRITE IT OUT 10 TIMES:

1 ....

....

2 ....

....

3 ....

....

4 ....

....

5 ....

....

6 ....

....

7 ....

....

8 ....

....

9 ....

....

10 ....

....

NOW REPEAT THIS THREE TIMES WITH YOUR HAND ON YOUR HEART:

♥♥♥

"I'M SO HAPPY AND GRATEFUL THAT I RECOGNISE HOW MUCH I REALLY DO MATTER."

♥♥♥

NOW WRITE HOW YOU FEEL AFTER COMPLETING THIS EXCERCISE. DOES IT BRING ANYTHING UP FOR YOU? HOW DO YOU WANT TO FEEL TODAY?

....

....

....

SAY THIS AFFIRMATION OUT LOUD WITH YOUR HAND ON YOUR HEART:

NOW WRITE IT OUT 10 TIMES:

1 ....

....

2 ....

....

3 ....

....

4 ....

....

5 ....

....

6 ....

....

7 ....

....

8 ....

....

9 ....

....

10 ....

....

NOW REPEAT THIS THREE TIMES WITH YOUR HAND ON YOUR HEART:

♥♥♥

"I LOVE THE IDEA THAT I'M PERFECT JUST AS I AM.
IT LIBERATES ME."

♥♥♥

NOW WRITE HOW YOU FEEL AFTER COMPLETING THIS EXCERCISE. DOES IT BRING ANYTHING UP FOR YOU? HOW DO YOU WANT TO FEEL TODAY?

....

....

....

SAY THIS AFFIRMATION OUT LOUD WITH YOUR HAND ON YOUR HEART:

NOW WRITE IT OUT 10 TIMES:

1 ....

....

2 ....

....

3 ....

....

4 ....

....

5 ....

....

6 ....

....

7 ....

....

8 ....

....

9 ....

....

10 ....

....

NOW REPEAT THIS THREE TIMES WITH YOUR HAND ON YOUR HEART:

♥♥♥

"I'M GRATEFUL I HAVE THE CAPACITY TO FORGIVE MYSELF AND MOVE ON WITH EASE."

♥♥♥

NOW WRITE HOW YOU FEEL AFTER COMPLETING THIS EXCERCISE. DOES IT BRING ANYTHING UP FOR YOU? HOW DO YOU WANT TO FEEL TODAY?

....

....

....

SAY THIS AFFIRMATION OUT LOUD WITH YOUR HAND ON YOUR HEART:

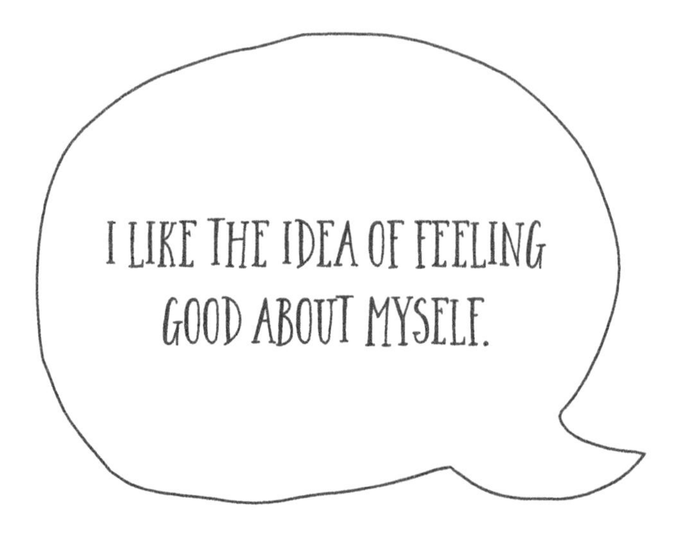

NOW WRITE IT OUT 10 TIMES:

1 ....

....

2 ....

....

3 ....

....

4 ....

....

5 ....

....

6 ....

....

7 ....

....

8 ....

....

9 ....

....

10 ....

....

NOW REPEAT THIS THREE TIMES WITH YOUR HAND ON YOUR HEART:

♥ ♥ ♥

"I ABSOLUTELY LOVE FEELING REALLY GOOD ABOUT MYSELF."

♥ ♥ ♥

NOW WRITE HOW YOU FEEL AFTER COMPLETING THIS EXCERCISE. DOES IT BRING ANYTHING UP FOR YOU? HOW DO YOU WANT TO FEEL TODAY?

....

....

....

Day 10

SAY THIS AFFIRMATION OUT LOUD WITH YOUR HAND ON YOUR HEART:

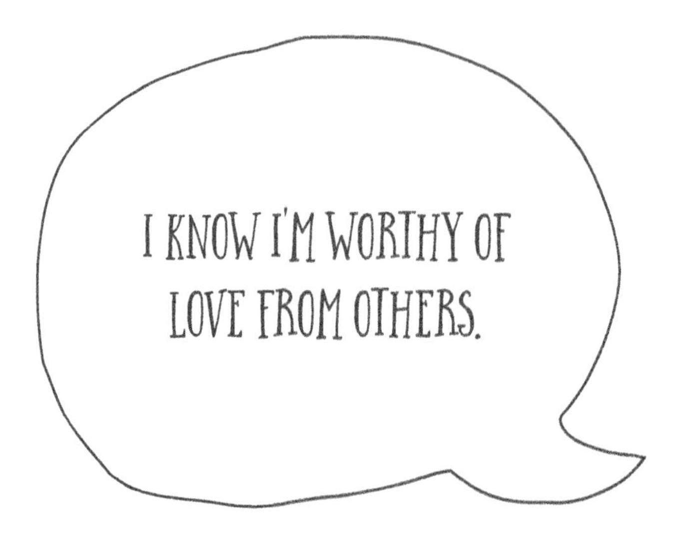

NOW WRITE IT OUT 10 TIMES:

1 ....

....

2 ....

....

3 ....

....

4 ....

....

5 ....

....

6 ....

....

7 ....

....

8 ....

....

9 ....

....

10 ....

....

NOW REPEAT THIS THREE TIMES WITH YOUR HAND ON YOUR HEART:

"I'M GRATEFUL TO KNOW THAT I'M WORTHY OF RECEIVING LOVE FROM OTHERS."

NOW WRITE HOW YOU FEEL AFTER COMPLETING THIS EXCERCISE. DOES IT BRING ANYTHING UP FOR YOU? HOW DO YOU WANT TO FEEL TODAY?

....

....

....

SAY THIS AFFIRMATION OUT LOUD WITH YOUR HAND ON YOUR HEART:

NOW WRITE IT OUT 10 TIMES:

1 ....

....

2 ....

....

3 ....

....

4 ....

....

5 ....

....

6 ....

....

7 ....

....

8 ....

....

9 ....

....

10 ....

....

NOW REPEAT THIS THREE TIMES WITH YOUR HAND ON YOUR HEART:

"I'M GRATEFUL I GET TO LOVE
MYSELF FIRST."

NOW WRITE HOW YOU FEEL AFTER COMPLETING THIS EXCERCISE. DOES IT BRING ANYTHING UP FOR YOU? HOW DO YOU WANT TO FEEL TODAY?

....

....

....

Day 12

SAY THIS AFFIRMATION OUT LOUD WITH YOUR HAND ON YOUR HEART:

NOW WRITE IT OUT 10 TIMES:

1 ....

....

2 ....

....

3 ....

....

4 ....

....

5 ....

....

6 ....

....

7 ....

....

8 ....

....

9 ....

....

10 ....

....

NOW REPEAT THIS THREE TIMES WITH YOUR HAND ON YOUR HEART:

♥♥♥

"I LOVE OPENING UP TO THE IDEA THAT I CAN LOVE MYSELF FULLY."

♥♥♥

NOW WRITE HOW YOU FEEL AFTER COMPLETING THIS EXCERCISE. DOES IT BRING ANYTHING UP FOR YOU? HOW DO YOU WANT TO FEEL TODAY?

....

....

....

Day 13

SAY THIS AFFIRMATION OUT LOUD WITH YOUR HAND ON YOUR HEART:

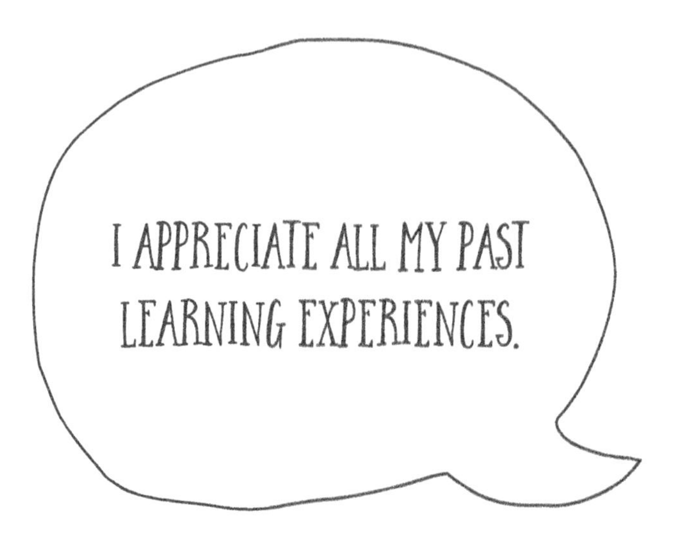

NOW WRITE IT OUT 10 TIMES:

1 ....

....

2 ....

....

3 ....

....

4 ....

....

5 ....

....

6 ....

....

7 ....

....

8 ....

....

9 ....

....

10 ....

....

NOW REPEAT THIS THREE TIMES WITH YOUR HAND ON YOUR HEART:

♥♥♥

"I SEND LOVE TO ALL THE EXPERIENCES IN MY PAST THAT HAVE HELPED ME TO LEARN AND GROW."

♥♥♥

NOW WRITE HOW YOU FEEL AFTER COMPLETING THIS EXCERCISE. DOES IT BRING ANYTHING UP FOR YOU? HOW DO YOU WANT TO FEEL TODAY?

....

....

....

Day 14

SAY THIS AFFIRMATION OUT LOUD WITH YOUR HAND ON YOUR HEART:

NOW WRITE IT OUT 10 TIMES:

1 ....

....

2 ....

....

3 ....

....

4 ....

....

5 ....

....

6 ....

....

7 ....

....

8 ....

....

9 ....

....

10 ....

....

NOW REPEAT THIS THREE TIMES WITH YOUR HAND ON YOUR HEART:

♥ ♥ ♥

"I LOVE KNOWING THAT I'M A GOOD PERSON. IT FILLS ME WITH CONFIDENCE AND I'M GRATEFUL FOR THAT."

♥ ♥ ♥

NOW WRITE HOW YOU FEEL AFTER COMPLETING THIS EXCERCISE. DOES IT BRING ANYTHING UP FOR YOU? HOW DO YOU WANT TO FEEL TODAY?

....

....

....

Day 15

SAY THIS AFFIRMATION OUT LOUD WITH YOUR HAND ON YOUR HEART:

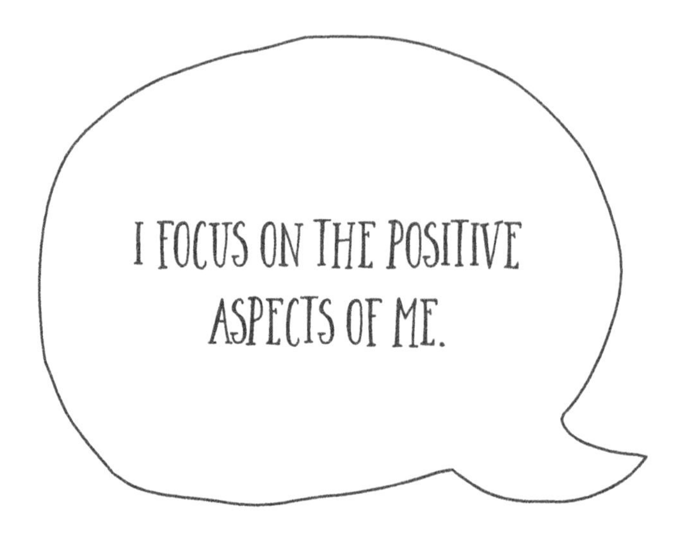

NOW WRITE IT OUT 10 TIMES:

1 ....

....

2 ....

....

3 ....

....

4 ....

....

5 ....

....

6

7

8

9

10

NOW REPEAT THIS THREE TIMES WITH YOUR HAND ON YOUR HEART:

"I APPRECIATE EVERY SINGLE POSITIVE THING ABOUT MYSELF, BIG OR SMALL."

NOW WRITE HOW YOU FEEL AFTER COMPLETING THIS EXCERCISE. DOES IT BRING ANYTHING UP FOR YOU? HOW DO YOU WANT TO FEEL TODAY?

Day 16

SAY THIS AFFIRMATION OUT LOUD WITH YOUR HAND ON YOUR HEART:

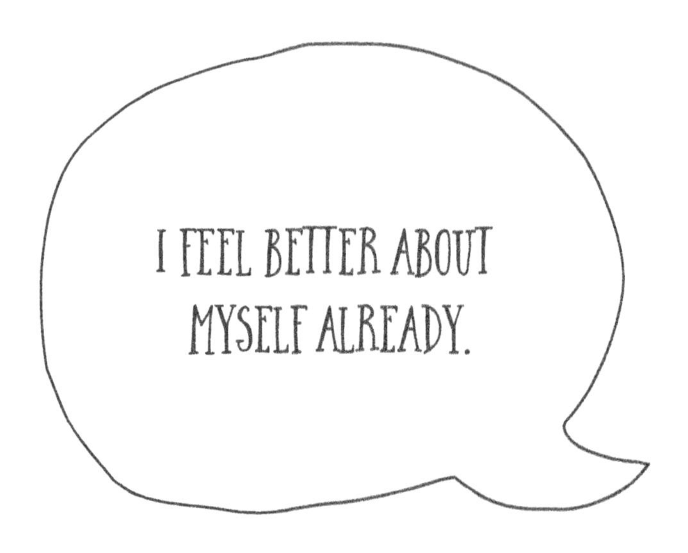

NOW WRITE IT OUT 10 TIMES:

1 ....

....

2 ....

....

3 ....

....

4 ....

....

5 ....

....

6 ....

....

7 ....

....

8 ....

....

9 ....

....

10 ....

....

NOW REPEAT THIS THREE TIMES WITH YOUR HAND ON YOUR HEART:

♥♥♥

"I'M SO HAPPY THAT I'M ALREADY FEELING BETTER ABOUT MYSELF."

♥♥♥

NOW WRITE HOW YOU FEEL AFTER COMPLETING THIS EXCERCISE. DOES IT BRING ANYTHING UP FOR YOU? HOW DO YOU WANT TO FEEL TODAY?

....

....

....

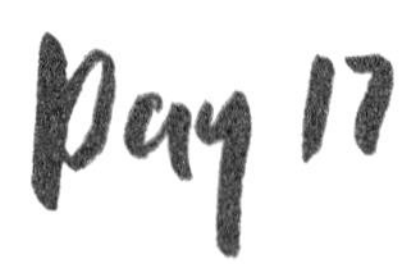

SAY THIS AFFIRMATION OUT LOUD WITH YOUR HAND ON YOUR HEART:

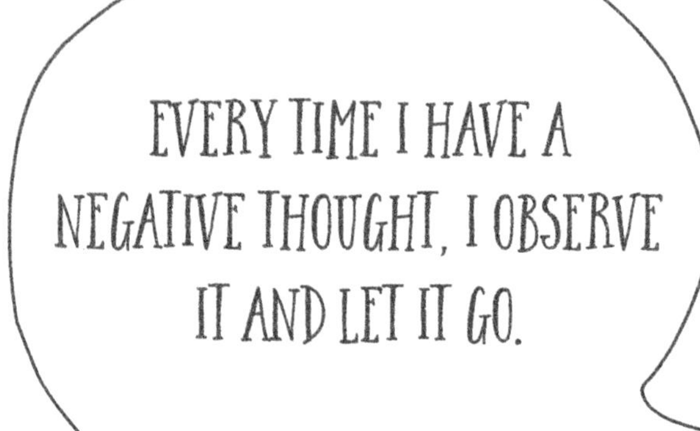

NOW WRITE IT OUT 10 TIMES:

1 ....

....

2 ....

....

3 ....

....

4 ....

....

5 ....

....

6 ....

....

7 ....

....

8 ....

....

9 ....

....

10 ....

....

NOW REPEAT THIS THREE TIMES WITH YOUR HAND ON YOUR HEART:

♥♥♥

"I'M GRATEFUL THAT I NO LONGER ATTACH MEANING TO MY NEGATIVE THOUGHTS AND LET THEM GO."

♥♥♥

NOW WRITE HOW YOU FEEL AFTER COMPLETING THIS EXCERCISE. DOES IT BRING ANYTHING UP FOR YOU? HOW DO YOU WANT TO FEEL TODAY?

....

....

....

SAY THIS AFFIRMATION OUT LOUD WITH YOUR HAND ON YOUR HEART:

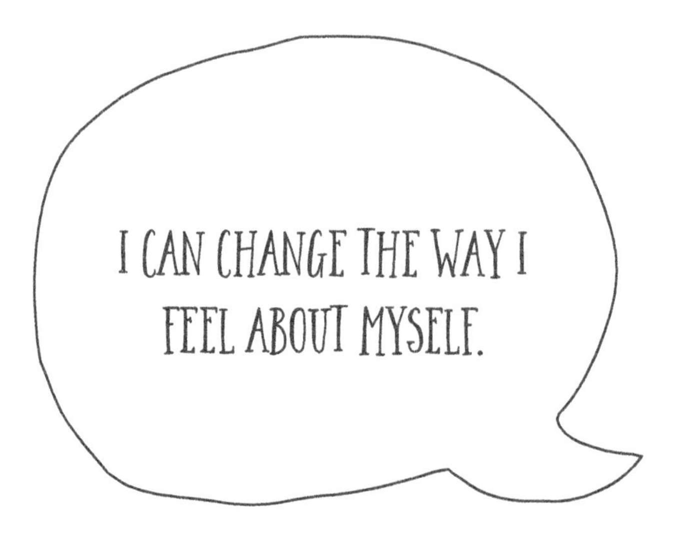

NOW WRITE IT OUT 10 TIMES:

1 ....

....

2 ....

....

3 ....

....

4 ....

....

5 ....

....

6 ....

....

7 ....

....

8 ....

....

9 ....

....

10 ....

....

NOW REPEAT THIS THREE TIMES WITH YOUR HAND ON YOUR HEART:

♥♥♥

"I SEND LOVE AND GRATITUDE TO THE NEW FEELINGS I'M CREATING ABOUT MYSELF."

NOW WRITE HOW YOU FEEL AFTER COMPLETING THIS EXCERCISE. DOES IT BRING ANYTHING UP FOR YOU? HOW DO YOU WANT TO FEEL TODAY?

....

....

....

SAY THIS AFFIRMATION OUT LOUD WITH YOUR HAND ON YOUR HEART:

NOW WRITE IT OUT 10 TIMES:

1 ....

....

2 ....

....

3 ....

....

4 ....

....

5 ....

....

6 ....

....

7 ....

....

8 ....

....

9 ....

....

10 ....

....

NOW REPEAT THIS THREE TIMES WITH YOUR HAND ON YOUR HEART:

"I'M GRATEFUL FOR MY GOOD QUALITIES AND CELEBRATE THEM EVERY DAY."

NOW WRITE HOW YOU FEEL AFTER COMPLETING THIS EXCERCISE. DOES IT BRING ANYTHING UP FOR YOU? HOW DO YOU WANT TO FEEL TODAY?

....

....

....

Day 20

SAY THIS AFFIRMATION OUT LOUD WITH YOUR HAND ON YOUR HEART:

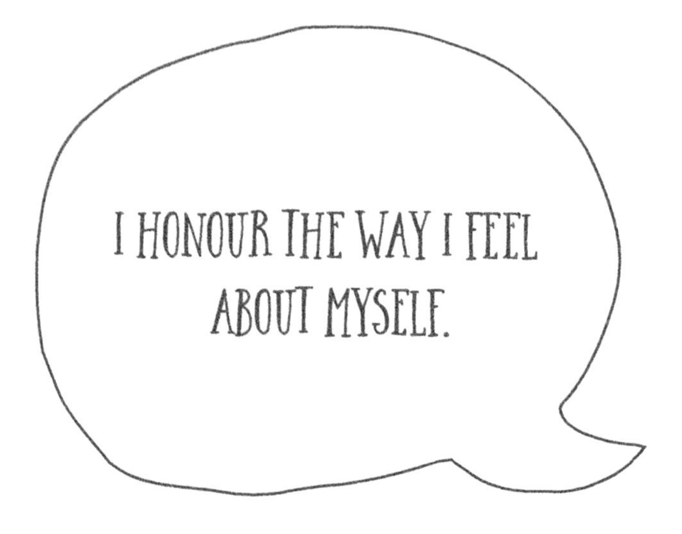

NOW WRITE IT OUT 10 TIMES:

1 ....

....

2 ....

....

3 ....

....

4 ....

....

5 ....

....

6 ....

....

7 ....

....

8 ....

....

9 ....

....

10 ....

....

NOW REPEAT THIS THREE TIMES WITH YOUR HAND ON YOUR HEART:

♥♥♥

"I REALLY APPRECIATE MYSELF AND IMPROVE THE WAY I FEEL."

♥♥♥

NOW WRITE HOW YOU FEEL AFTER COMPLETING THIS EXCERCISE. DOES IT BRING ANYTHING UP FOR YOU? HOW DO YOU WANT TO FEEL TODAY?

....

....

....

SAY THIS AFFIRMATION OUT LOUD WITH YOUR HAND ON YOUR HEART:

NOW WRITE IT OUT 10 TIMES:

1 ....

....

2 ....

....

3 ....

....

4 ....

....

5 ....

....

6 ....

....

7 ....

....

8 ....

....

9 ....

....

10 ....

....

NOW REPEAT THIS THREE TIMES WITH YOUR HAND ON YOUR HEART:

♥♥♥

"I'M GRATEFUL THAT I'M MOVING FROM FEAR TO LOVE."

♥♥♥

NOW WRITE HOW YOU FEEL AFTER COMPLETING THIS EXCERCISE. DOES IT BRING ANYTHING UP FOR YOU? HOW DO YOU WANT TO FEEL TODAY?

....

....

....

SAY THIS AFFIRMATION OUT LOUD WITH YOUR HAND ON YOUR HEART:

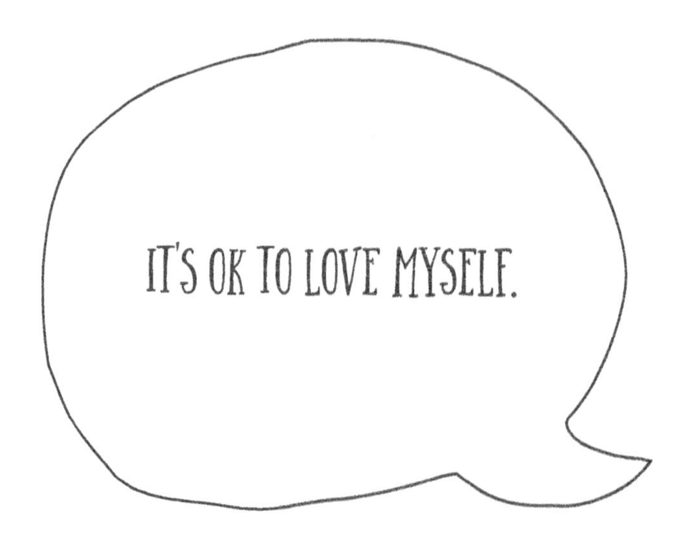

NOW WRITE IT OUT 10 TIMES:

1 ....

....

2 ....

....

3 ....

....

4 ....

....

5 ....

....

6 ....

....

7 ....

....

8 ....

....

9 ....

....

10 ....

....

NOW REPEAT THIS THREE TIMES WITH YOUR HAND ON YOUR HEART:

♥♥♥

"I'M SO HAPPY AND GRATEFUL NOW THAT I KNOW IT'S OK FOR ME TO LOVE ME."

♥♥♥

NOW WRITE HOW YOU FEEL AFTER COMPLETING THIS EXCERCISE. DOES IT BRING ANYTHING UP FOR YOU? HOW DO YOU WANT TO FEEL TODAY?

....

....

....

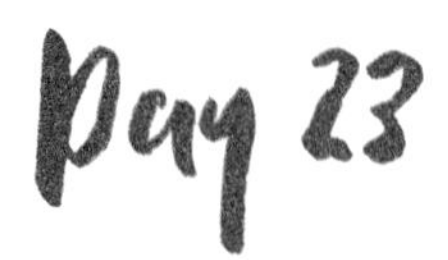

SAY THIS AFFIRMATION OUT LOUD WITH YOUR HAND ON YOUR HEART:

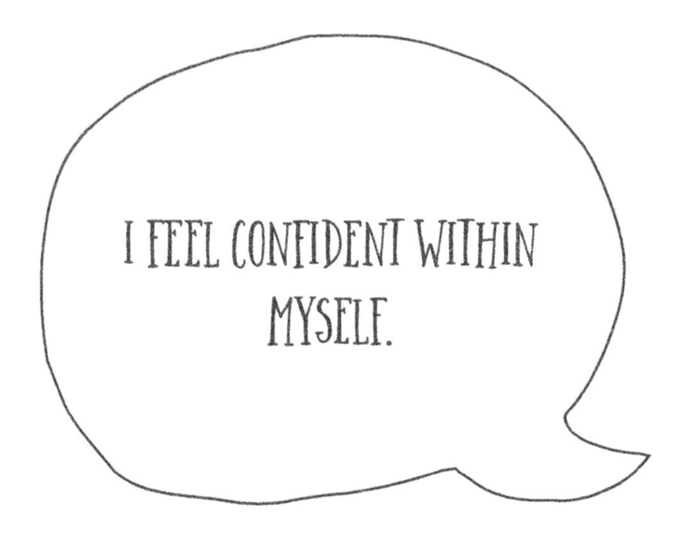

NOW WRITE IT OUT 10 TIMES:

1 ....

....

2 ....

....

3 ....

....

4 ....

....

5 ....

....

6 ....

....

7 ....

....

8 ....

....

9 ....

....

10 ....

....

NOW REPEAT THIS THREE TIMES WITH YOUR HAND ON YOUR HEART:

♥♥♥

"I LOVE FEELING CONFIDENT WITHIN MYSELF. IT STARTS WITHIN ME FIRST."

♥♥♥

NOW WRITE HOW YOU FEEL AFTER COMPLETING THIS EXCERCISE. DOES IT BRING ANYTHING UP FOR YOU? HOW DO YOU WANT TO FEEL TODAY?

....

....

....

SAY THIS AFFIRMATION OUT LOUD WITH YOUR HAND ON YOUR HEART:

NOW WRITE IT OUT 10 TIMES:

1 ....

....

2 ....

....

3 ....

....

4 ....

....

5 ....

....

6

7

8

9

10

NOW REPEAT THIS THREE TIMES WITH YOUR HAND ON YOUR HEART:

"I LOVE OWNING MY OWN POWER.
I APPRECIATE IT IMMENSELY."

NOW WRITE HOW YOU FEEL AFTER COMPLETING THIS EXCERCISE. DOES IT BRING ANYTHING UP FOR YOU? HOW DO YOU WANT TO FEEL TODAY?

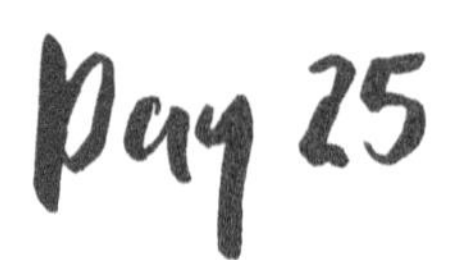

SAY THIS AFFIRMATION OUT LOUD WITH YOUR HAND ON YOUR HEART:

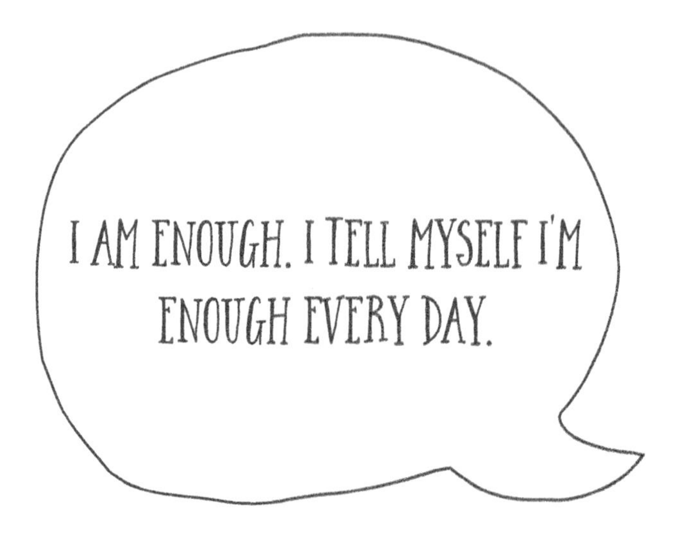

NOW WRITE IT OUT 10 TIMES:

1 ....

....

2 ....

....

3 ....

....

4 ....

....

5 ....

....

6 ....

....

7 ....

....

8 ....

....

9 ....

....

10 ....

....

NOW REPEAT THIS THREE TIMES WITH YOUR HAND ON YOUR HEART:

♥♥♥

"I'M SO GRATEFUL THAT I KNOW I'M ENOUGH. I LOVE TRAINING MY MIND TO BELIEVE THAT."

♥♥♥

NOW WRITE HOW YOU FEEL AFTER COMPLETING THIS EXCERCISE. DOES IT BRING ANYTHING UP FOR YOU? HOW DO YOU WANT TO FEEL TODAY?

....

....

....

Day 26

SAY THIS AFFIRMATION OUT LOUD WITH YOUR HAND ON YOUR HEART:

NOW WRITE IT OUT 10 TIMES:

1 ....

....

2 ....

....

3 ....

....

4 ....

....

5 ....

....

6 ....

....

7 ....

....

8 ....

....

9 ....

....

10 ....

....

NOW REPEAT THIS THREE TIMES WITH YOUR HAND ON YOUR HEART:

♥♥♥

"I LOVE AND APPRECIATE KNOWING THAT I'M PERFECT JUST AS I AM."

♥♥♥

NOW WRITE HOW YOU FEEL AFTER COMPLETING THIS EXCERCISE. DOES IT BRING ANYTHING UP FOR YOU? HOW DO YOU WANT TO FEEL TODAY?

....

....

....

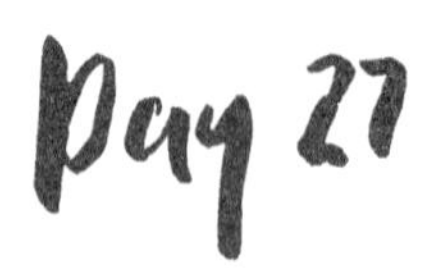

Day 27

SAY THIS AFFIRMATION OUT LOUD WITH YOUR HAND ON YOUR HEART:

NOW WRITE IT OUT 10 TIMES:

1 ....

....

2 ....

....

3 ....

....

4 ....

....

5 ....

....

6 ....

....

7 ....

....

8 ....

....

9 ....

....

10 ....

....

NOW REPEAT THIS THREE TIMES WITH YOUR HAND ON YOUR HEART:

♥♥♥

"I LOVE BEING A POWERFUL FORCE FOR GOOD."

♥♥♥

NOW WRITE HOW YOU FEEL AFTER COMPLETING THIS EXCERCISE. DOES IT BRING ANYTHING UP FOR YOU? HOW DO YOU WANT TO FEEL TODAY?

....

....

....

SAY THIS AFFIRMATION OUT LOUD WITH YOUR HAND ON YOUR HEART:

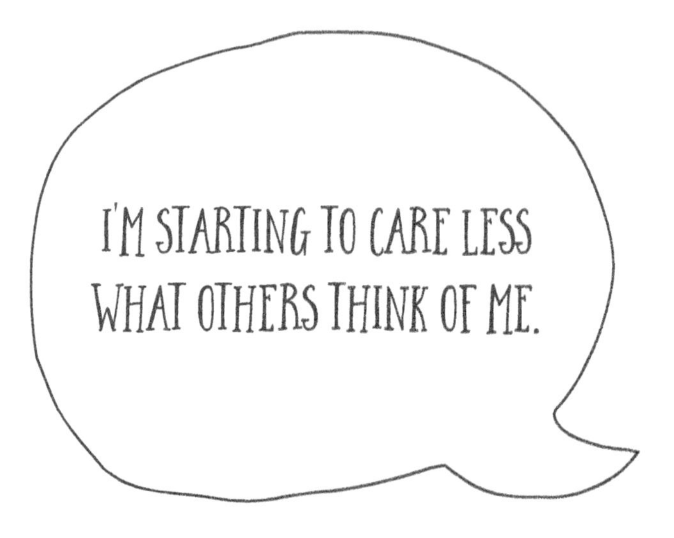

NOW WRITE IT OUT 10 TIMES:

1 ....

....

2 ....

....

3 ....

....

4 ....

....

5 ....

....

6 ....

....

7 ....

....

8 ....

....

9 ....

....

10 ....

....

NOW REPEAT THIS THREE TIMES WITH YOUR HAND ON YOUR HEART:

♥♥♥

"I APPRECIATE MYSELF AND DON'T NEED OTHER PEOPLE'S APPROVAL."

♥♥♥

NOW WRITE HOW YOU FEEL AFTER COMPLETING THIS EXCERCISE. DOES IT BRING ANYTHING UP FOR YOU? HOW DO YOU WANT TO FEEL TODAY?

....

....

....

SAY THIS AFFIRMATION OUT LOUD WITH YOUR HAND ON YOUR HEART:

NOW WRITE IT OUT 10 TIMES:

1 ....

....

2 ....

....

3 ....

....

4 ....

....

5 ....

....

6 ....

....

7 ....

....

8 ....

....

9 ....

....

10 ....

....

NOW REPEAT THIS THREE TIMES WITH YOUR HAND ON YOUR HEART:

♥♥♥

"I APPRECIATE EVERY 'MISTAKE' I'VE MADE, KNOWING IT WAS NEVER REALLY A MISTAKE."

♥♥♥

NOW WRITE HOW YOU FEEL AFTER COMPLETING THIS EXCERCISE. DOES IT BRING ANYTHING UP FOR YOU? HOW DO YOU WANT TO FEEL TODAY?

....

....

....

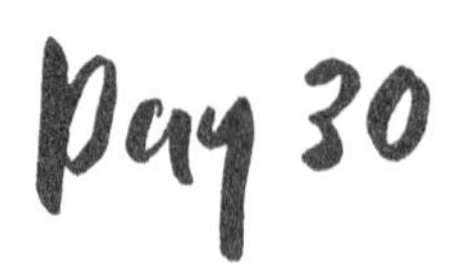

Day 30

SAY THIS AFFIRMATION OUT LOUD WITH YOUR HAND ON YOUR HEART:

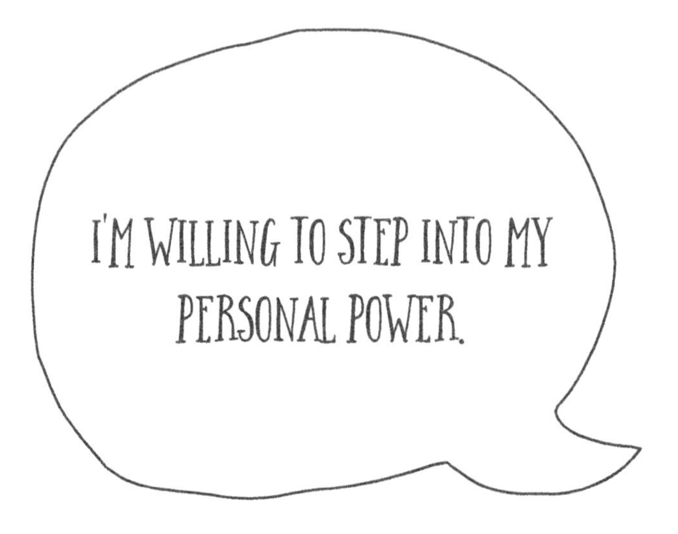

NOW WRITE IT OUT 10 TIMES:

1 ....

....

2 ....

....

3 ....

....

4 ....

....

5 ....

....

6 ....

....

7 ....

....

8 ....

....

9 ....

....

10 ....

....

NOW REPEAT THIS THREE TIMES WITH YOUR HAND ON YOUR HEART:

♥♥♥

"I GET EXCITED ABOUT MY PERSONAL POWER.
I SEND MYSELF FEELINGS OF LOVE AND GRACE."

♥♥♥

NOW WRITE HOW YOU FEEL AFTER COMPLETING THIS EXCERCISE. DOES IT BRING ANYTHING UP FOR YOU? HOW DO YOU WANT TO FEEL TODAY?

....

....

....

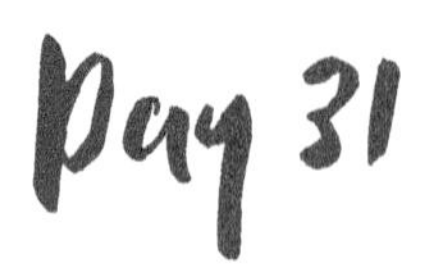

SAY THIS AFFIRMATION OUT LOUD WITH YOUR HAND ON YOUR HEART:

NOW WRITE IT OUT 10 TIMES:

1 ....

....

2 ....

....

3 ....

....

4 ....

....

5 ....

....

6 ....

....

7 ....

....

8 ....

....

9 ....

....

10 ....

....

NOW REPEAT THIS THREE TIMES WITH YOUR HAND ON YOUR HEART:

♥♥♥

"I AM SO HAPPY AND GRATEFUL THAT I HAVE AN INNER SPARKLE!."

♥♥♥

NOW WRITE HOW YOU FEEL AFTER COMPLETING THIS EXCERCISE. DOES IT BRING ANYTHING UP FOR YOU? HOW DO YOU WANT TO FEEL TODAY?

....

....

....

Day 32

SAY THIS AFFIRMATION OUT LOUD WITH YOUR HAND ON YOUR HEART:

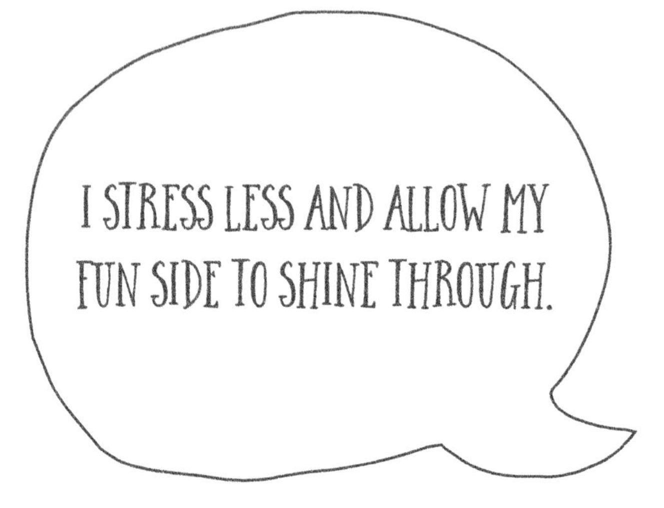

NOW WRITE IT OUT 10 TIMES:

1 ....

....

2 ....

....

3 ....

....

4 ....

....

5 ....

....

6 ....

....

7 ....

....

8 ....

....

9 ....

....

10 ....

....

NOW REPEAT THIS THREE TIMES WITH YOUR HAND ON YOUR HEART:

"I LOVE ALLOWING MY FUN SIDE TO SHOW.
IT LIGHTENS MY ENERGY."

NOW WRITE HOW YOU FEEL AFTER COMPLETING THIS EXCERCISE. DOES IT BRING ANYTHING UP FOR YOU? HOW DO YOU WANT TO FEEL TODAY?

....

....

....

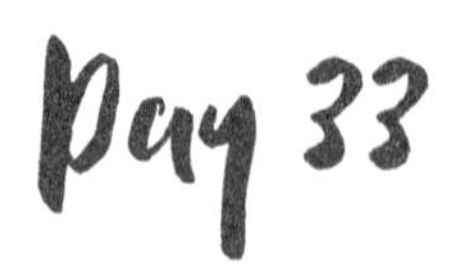

SAY THIS AFFIRMATION OUT LOUD WITH YOUR HAND ON YOUR HEART:

NOW WRITE IT OUT 10 TIMES:

1 ....

....

2 ....

....

3 ....

....

4 ....

....

5 ....

....

6 ....

....

7 ....

....

8 ....

....

9 ....

....

10 ....

....

NOW REPEAT THIS THREE TIMES WITH YOUR HAND ON YOUR HEART:

♥♥♥

"I LOVE ALLOWING MY LIGHT TO SHINE.
I LET IT SHINE BRIGHT!"

♥♥♥

NOW WRITE HOW YOU FEEL AFTER COMPLETING THIS EXCERCISE. DOES IT BRING ANYTHING UP FOR YOU? HOW DO YOU WANT TO FEEL TODAY?

....

....

....

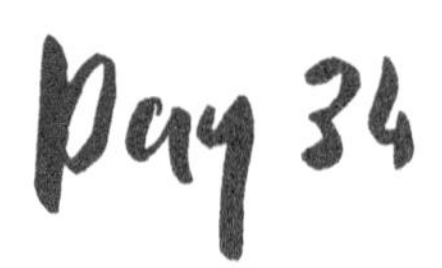

SAY THIS AFFIRMATION OUT LOUD WITH YOUR HAND ON YOUR HEART:

NOW WRITE IT OUT 10 TIMES:

1 ....

....

2 ....

....

3 ....

....

4 ....

....

5 ....

....

6 ....

....

7 ....

....

8 ....

....

9 ....

....

10 ....

....

NOW REPEAT THIS THREE TIMES WITH YOUR HAND ON YOUR HEART:

"I LOVE ALLOWING MY LIGHT TO TOUCH THE HEARTS OF OTHERS."

NOW WRITE HOW YOU FEEL AFTER COMPLETING THIS EXCERCISE. DOES IT BRING ANYTHING UP FOR YOU? HOW DO YOU WANT TO FEEL TODAY?

....

....

....

Day 35

SAY THIS AFFIRMATION OUT LOUD WITH YOUR HAND ON YOUR HEART:

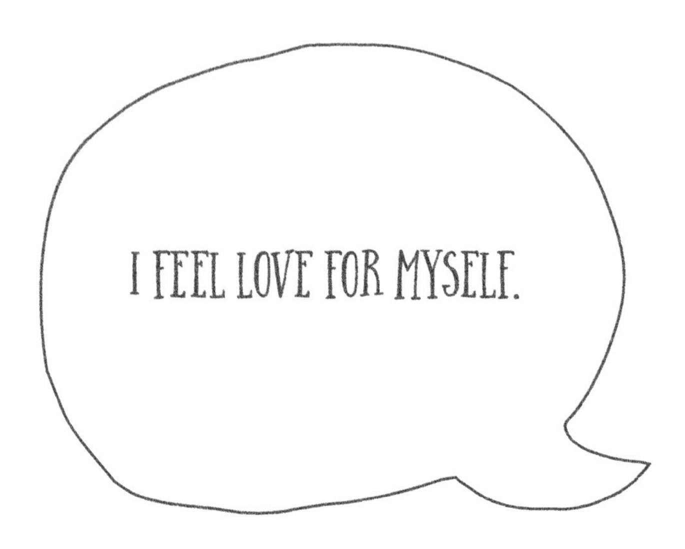

NOW WRITE IT OUT 10 TIMES:

1 ....

....

2 ....

....

3 ....

....

4 ....

....

5 ....

....

6 ....

....

7 ....

....

8 ....

....

9 ....

....

10 ....

....

NOW REPEAT THIS THREE TIMES WITH YOUR HAND ON YOUR HEART:

♥♥♥

"I'M GRATEFUL THAT EVERY DAY I GET TO FEEL MORE LOVE FOR MYSELF."

♥♥♥

NOW WRITE HOW YOU FEEL AFTER COMPLETING THIS EXCERCISE. DOES IT BRING ANYTHING UP FOR YOU? HOW DO YOU WANT TO FEEL TODAY?

....

....

....

Day 36

SAY THIS AFFIRMATION OUT LOUD WITH YOUR HAND ON YOUR HEART:

NOW WRITE IT OUT 10 TIMES:

1 ....

....

2 ....

....

3 ....

....

4 ....

....

5 ....

....

6 ....

....

7 ....

....

8 ....

....

9 ....

....

10 ....

....

NOW REPEAT THIS THREE TIMES WITH YOUR HAND ON YOUR HEART:

♥♥♥

"I APPRECIATE BEING ABLE TO HELP AND FEEL FOR OTHERS. I LOVE TO SHOW THEM LOVE."

♥♥♥

NOW WRITE HOW YOU FEEL AFTER COMPLETING THIS EXCERCISE. DOES IT BRING ANYTHING UP FOR YOU? HOW DO YOU WANT TO FEEL TODAY?

....

....

....

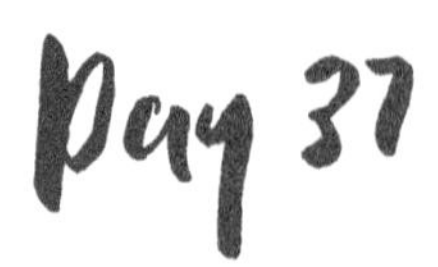

SAY THIS AFFIRMATION OUT LOUD WITH YOUR HAND ON YOUR HEART:

NOW WRITE IT OUT 10 TIMES:

1 ....

....

2 ....

....

3 ....

....

4 ....

....

5 ....

....

6 ....

....

7 ....

....

8 ....

....

9 ....

....

10 ....

....

NOW REPEAT THIS THREE TIMES WITH YOUR HAND ON YOUR HEART:

♥♥♥

"I SEND LOVE AND GRATITUDE TO MYSELF AND DO WHAT'S BEST FOR ME."

♥♥♥

NOW WRITE HOW YOU FEEL AFTER COMPLETING THIS EXCERCISE. DOES IT BRING ANYTHING UP FOR YOU? HOW DO YOU WANT TO FEEL TODAY?

....

....

....

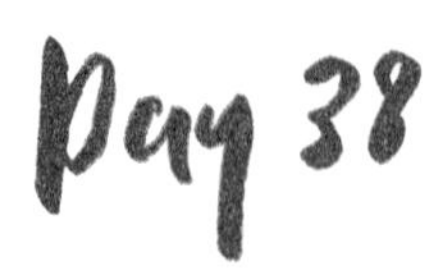

SAY THIS AFFIRMATION OUT LOUD WITH YOUR HAND ON YOUR HEART:

NOW WRITE IT OUT 10 TIMES:

1 ....

....

2 ....

....

3 ....

....

4 ....

....

5 ....

....

6 ....

....

7 ....

....

8 ....

....

9 ....

....

10 ....

....

NOW REPEAT THIS THREE TIMES WITH YOUR HAND ON YOUR HEART:

♥♥♥

"I GRATEFULLY SEND LOVE OUT AND RECEIVE IT BACK."

♥♥♥

NOW WRITE HOW YOU FEEL AFTER COMPLETING THIS EXCERCISE. DOES IT BRING ANYTHING UP FOR YOU? HOW DO YOU WANT TO FEEL TODAY?

....

....

....

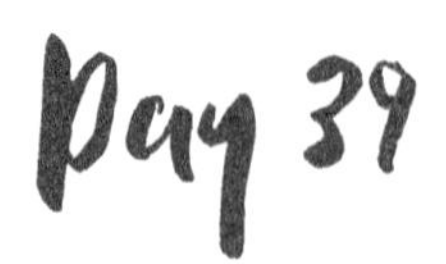

SAY THIS AFFIRMATION OUT LOUD WITH YOUR HAND ON YOUR HEART:

NOW WRITE IT OUT 10 TIMES:

1 ....

....

2 ....

....

3 ....

....

4 ....

....

5 ....

....

6 ....

....

7 ....

....

8 ....

....

9 ....

....

10 ....

....

NOW REPEAT THIS THREE TIMES WITH YOUR HAND ON YOUR HEART:

♥♥♥

"I APPRECIATE THE LOVE I RECEIVE, KNOWING IT IS SAFE TO HAVE."

♥♥♥

NOW WRITE HOW YOU FEEL AFTER COMPLETING THIS EXCERCISE. DOES IT BRING ANYTHING UP FOR YOU? HOW DO YOU WANT TO FEEL TODAY?

....

....

....

SAY THIS AFFIRMATION OUT LOUD WITH YOUR HAND ON YOUR HEART:

NOW WRITE IT OUT 10 TIMES:

1 ....

....

2 ....

....

3 ....

....

4 ....

....

5 ....

....

6 ....

....

7 ....

....

8 ....

....

9 ....

....

10 ....

....

NOW REPEAT THIS THREE TIMES WITH YOUR HAND ON YOUR HEART:

♥ ♥ ♥

"I'M GRATEFUL THAT THE BLOCKS TO LOVING MYSELF ARE CLEARING VERY QUICKLY."

♥ ♥ ♥

NOW WRITE HOW YOU FEEL AFTER COMPLETING THIS EXCERCISE. DOES IT BRING ANYTHING UP FOR YOU? HOW DO YOU WANT TO FEEL TODAY?

....

....

....

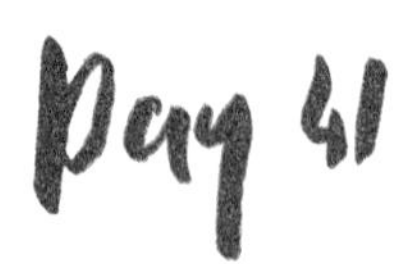

SAY THIS AFFIRMATION OUT LOUD WITH YOUR HAND ON YOUR HEART:

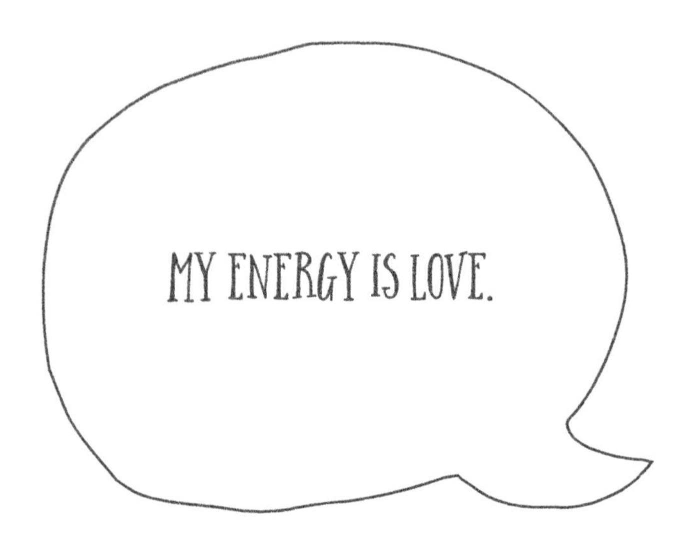

NOW WRITE IT OUT 10 TIMES:

1 ....

....

2 ....

....

3 ....

....

4 ....

....

5 ....

....

6 ....

....

7 ....

....

8 ....

....

9 ....

....

10 ....

....

NOW REPEAT THIS THREE TIMES WITH YOUR HAND ON YOUR HEART:

♥♥♥

"I'M SO HAPPY AND GRATEFUL I HAVE ALIGNED MY ENERGY WITH LOVE."

♥♥♥

NOW WRITE HOW YOU FEEL AFTER COMPLETING THIS EXCERCISE. DOES IT BRING ANYTHING UP FOR YOU? HOW DO YOU WANT TO FEEL TODAY?

....

....

....

SAY THIS AFFIRMATION OUT LOUD WITH YOUR HAND ON YOUR HEART:

NOW WRITE IT OUT 10 TIMES:

1 ....

....

2 ....

....

3 ....

....

4 ....

....

5 ....

....

6 ....

....

7 ....

....

8 ....

....

9 ....

....

10 ....

....

NOW REPEAT THIS THREE TIMES WITH YOUR HAND ON YOUR HEART:

"I AM THANKFUL THAT I SHARE LOVE,
I RECEIVE LOVE, I AM LOVE."

NOW WRITE HOW YOU FEEL AFTER COMPLETING THIS EXCERCISE. DOES IT BRING ANYTHING UP FOR YOU? HOW DO YOU WANT TO FEEL TODAY?

....

....

....

SAY THIS AFFIRMATION OUT LOUD WITH YOUR HAND ON YOUR HEART:

NOW WRITE IT OUT 10 TIMES:

1 ....

....

2 ....

....

3 ....

....

4 ....

....

5 ....

....

6 ....

....

7 ....

....

8 ....

....

9 ....

....

10 ....

....

NOW REPEAT THIS THREE TIMES WITH YOUR HAND ON YOUR HEART:

♥♥♥

"I AM GRATEFUL THAT I AM A JOYFUL SOUL. OTHER PEOPLE PICK UP ON MY JOY AND IT EXPANDS."

♥♥♥

NOW WRITE HOW YOU FEEL AFTER COMPLETING THIS EXCERCISE. DOES IT BRING ANYTHING UP FOR YOU? HOW DO YOU WANT TO FEEL TODAY?

....

....

....

Day 44

SAY THIS AFFIRMATION OUT LOUD WITH YOUR HAND ON YOUR HEART:

NOW WRITE IT OUT 10 TIMES:

1 ....

....

2 ....

....

3 ....

....

4 ....

....

5 ....

....

6 ....

....

7 ....

....

8 ....

....

9 ....

....

10 ....

....

NOW REPEAT THIS THREE TIMES WITH YOUR HAND ON YOUR HEART:

♥♥♥

"I GIVE THANKS FOR MY POWER TO OVERCOME ANYTHING."

♥♥♥

NOW WRITE HOW YOU FEEL AFTER COMPLETING THIS EXCERCISE. DOES IT BRING ANYTHING UP FOR YOU? HOW DO YOU WANT TO FEEL TODAY?

....

....

....

SAY THIS AFFIRMATION OUT LOUD WITH YOUR HAND ON YOUR HEART:

NOW WRITE IT OUT 10 TIMES:

1 ....

....

2 ....

....

3 ....

....

4 ....

....

5 ....

....

6 ....

....

7 ....

....

8 ....

....

9 ....

....

10 ....

....

NOW REPEAT THIS THREE TIMES WITH YOUR HAND ON YOUR HEART:

♥♥♥

"I LOVE THAT FEELING I GET WHEN I BELIEVE IN MYSELF. I LOVE KNOWING I'M INDESTRUCTABLE."

♥♥♥

NOW WRITE HOW YOU FEEL AFTER COMPLETING THIS EXCERCISE. DOES IT BRING ANYTHING UP FOR YOU? HOW DO YOU WANT TO FEEL TODAY?

....

....

....

Day 46

SAY THIS AFFIRMATION OUT LOUD WITH YOUR HAND ON YOUR HEART:

NOW WRITE IT OUT 10 TIMES:

1 ....

....

2 ....

....

3 ....

....

4 ....

....

5 ....

....

6 ....

....

7 ....

....

8 ....

....

9 ....

....

10 ....

....

NOW REPEAT THIS THREE TIMES WITH YOUR HAND ON YOUR HEART:

♥♥♥

"I GRACIOUSLY INVITE MORE GENUINE LOVE INTO MY LIFE, WHATEVER FORM THAT TAKES."

♥♥♥

NOW WRITE HOW YOU FEEL AFTER COMPLETING THIS EXCERCISE. DOES IT BRING ANYTHING UP FOR YOU? HOW DO YOU WANT TO FEEL TODAY?

....

....

....

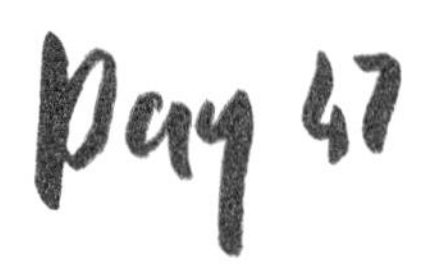

SAY THIS AFFIRMATION OUT LOUD WITH YOUR HAND ON YOUR HEART:

NOW WRITE IT OUT 10 TIMES:

1 ....

....

2 ....

....

3 ....

....

4 ....

....

5 ....

....

6 ....

....

7 ....

....

8 ....

....

9 ....

....

10 ....

....

NOW REPEAT THIS THREE TIMES WITH YOUR HAND ON YOUR HEART:

♥♥♥

"I'M GRATEFUL THAT I'M MOVING AWAY FROM MY FEAR OF BEING UNLOVEABLE."

♥♥♥

NOW WRITE HOW YOU FEEL AFTER COMPLETING THIS EXCERCISE. DOES IT BRING ANYTHING UP FOR YOU? HOW DO YOU WANT TO FEEL TODAY?

....

....

....

SAY THIS AFFIRMATION OUT LOUD WITH YOUR HAND ON YOUR HEART:

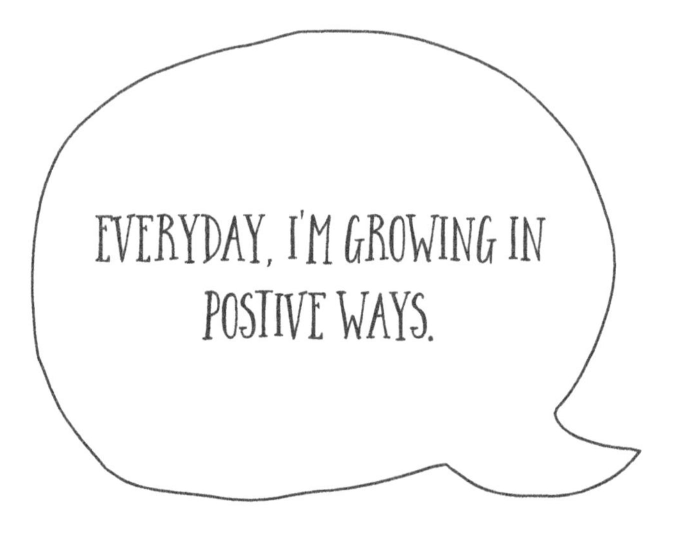

NOW WRITE IT OUT 10 TIMES:

1 ....

....

2 ....

....

3 ....

....

4 ....

....

5 ....

....

6 ....

....

7 ....

....

8 ....

....

9 ....

....

10 ....

....

NOW REPEAT THIS THREE TIMES WITH YOUR HAND ON YOUR HEART:

♥♥♥

"I'M GRATEFUL FOR ALL THE POSITIVE WAYS
IN WHICH I'M GROWING."

♥♥♥

NOW WRITE HOW YOU FEEL AFTER COMPLETING THIS EXCERCISE. DOES IT BRING ANYTHING UP FOR YOU? HOW DO YOU WANT TO FEEL TODAY?

....

....

....

SAY THIS AFFIRMATION OUT LOUD WITH YOUR HAND ON YOUR HEART:

NOW WRITE IT OUT 10 TIMES:

1 ....

....

2 ....

....

3 ....

....

4 ....

....

5 ....

....

6 ....

....

7 ....

....

8 ....

....

9 ....

....

10 ....

....

NOW REPEAT THIS THREE TIMES WITH YOUR HAND ON YOUR HEART:

♥♥♥

"I LOVE KNOWING THAT I LIGHT
UP OTHER PEOPLE'S LIVES."

♥♥♥

NOW WRITE HOW YOU FEEL AFTER COMPLETING THIS EXCERCISE. DOES IT BRING ANYTHING UP FOR YOU? HOW DO YOU WANT TO FEEL TODAY?

....

....

....

Day 50

SAY THIS AFFIRMATION OUT LOUD WITH YOUR HAND ON YOUR HEART:

NOW WRITE IT OUT 10 TIMES:

1 ....

....

2 ....

....

3 ....

....

4 ....

....

5 ....

....

6 ....

....

7 ....

....

8 ....

....

9 ....

....

10 ....

....

NOW REPEAT THIS THREE TIMES WITH YOUR HAND ON YOUR HEART:

♥♥♥

"I'M SO HAPPY AND GRATEFUL FOR THE STRENGTH I'M GAINING EVERY DAY."

♥♥♥

NOW WRITE HOW YOU FEEL AFTER COMPLETING THIS EXCERCISE. DOES IT BRING ANYTHING UP FOR YOU? HOW DO YOU WANT TO FEEL TODAY?

....

....

....

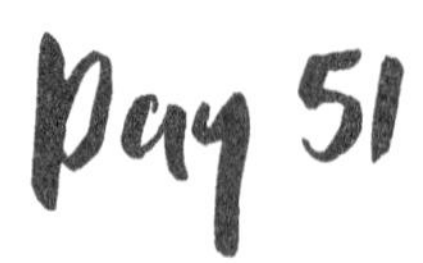

SAY THIS AFFIRMATION OUT LOUD WITH YOUR HAND ON YOUR HEART:

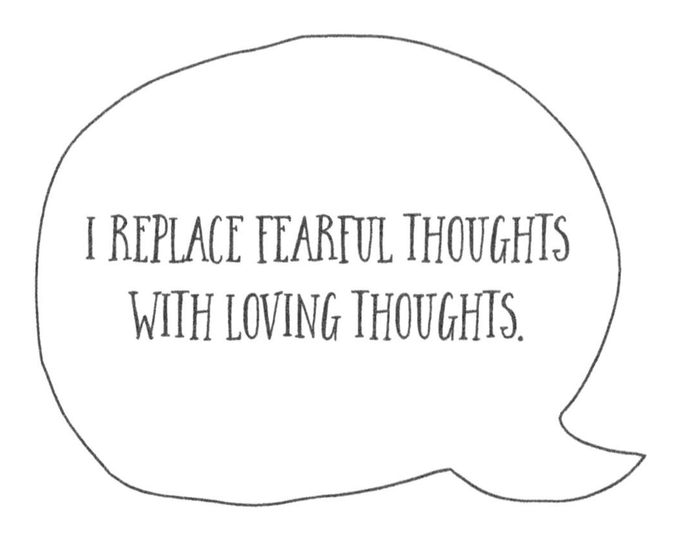

NOW WRITE IT OUT 10 TIMES:

1 ....

....

2 ....

....

3 ....

....

4 ....

....

5 ....

....

6 ....

....

7 ....

....

8 ....

....

9 ....

....

10 ....

....

NOW REPEAT THIS THREE TIMES WITH YOUR HAND ON YOUR HEART:

♥♥♥

"I'M HAPPY TO REPLACE FEARFUL THOUGHTS WITH LOVING THOUGHTS. I KNOW THEY SERVE ME WELL."

♥♥♥

NOW WRITE HOW YOU FEEL AFTER COMPLETING THIS EXCERCISE. DOES IT BRING ANYTHING UP FOR YOU? HOW DO YOU WANT TO FEEL TODAY?

....

....

....

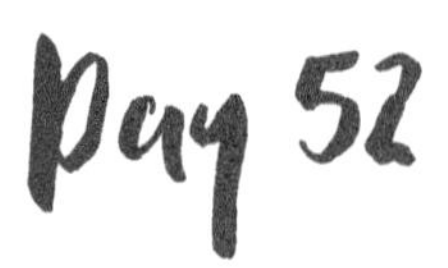

SAY THIS AFFIRMATION OUT LOUD WITH YOUR HAND ON YOUR HEART:

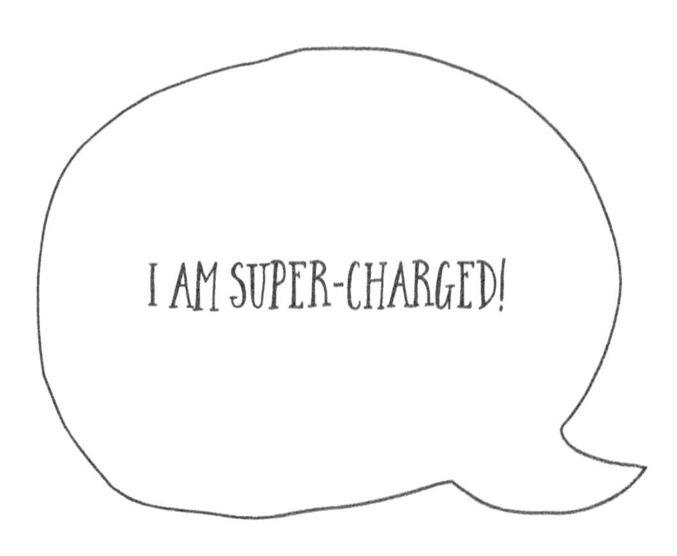

NOW WRITE IT OUT 10 TIMES:

1 ....

....

2 ....

....

3 ....

....

4 ....

....

5 ....

....

6 ....

....

7 ....

....

8 ....

....

9 ....

....

10 ....

....

NOW REPEAT THIS THREE TIMES WITH YOUR HAND ON YOUR HEART:

"I LOVE BEING SUPER-CHARGED! WHEN I'M SUPERCHARGED I CAN DO GREAT THINGS."

NOW WRITE HOW YOU FEEL AFTER COMPLETING THIS EXCERCISE. DOES IT BRING ANYTHING UP FOR YOU? HOW DO YOU WANT TO FEEL TODAY?

....

....

....

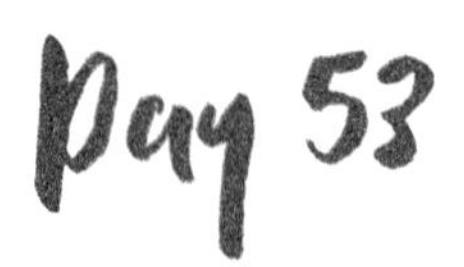

SAY THIS AFFIRMATION OUT LOUD WITH YOUR HAND ON YOUR HEART:

NOW WRITE IT OUT 10 TIMES:

1 ....

....

2 ....

....

3 ....

....

4 ....

....

5 ....

....

6 ....

....

7 ....

....

8 ....

....

9 ....

....

10 ....

....

NOW REPEAT THIS THREE TIMES WITH YOUR HAND ON YOUR HEART:

♥♥♥

"I'M SO HAPPY AND GRATEFUL FOR THE FUN I HAVE WHEN I'M BEING LOVING."

♥♥♥

NOW WRITE HOW YOU FEEL AFTER COMPLETING THIS EXCERCISE. DOES IT BRING ANYTHING UP FOR YOU? HOW DO YOU WANT TO FEEL TODAY?

....

....

....

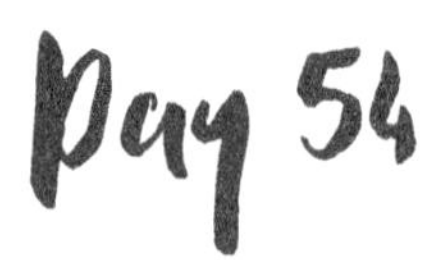

SAY THIS AFFIRMATION OUT LOUD WITH YOUR HAND ON YOUR HEART:

NOW WRITE IT OUT 10 TIMES:

1 ....

....

2 ....

....

3 ....

....

4 ....

....

5 ....

....

6 ....

....

7 ....

....

8 ....

....

9 ....

....

10 ....

....

NOW REPEAT THIS THREE TIMES WITH YOUR HAND ON YOUR HEART:

♥♥♥

"I'M GRATEFUL THAT I CAN OBSERVE MY NEGATIVE THOUGHTS AND LET THEM DRIFT AWAY."

♥♥♥

NOW WRITE HOW YOU FEEL AFTER COMPLETING THIS EXCERCISE. DOES IT BRING ANYTHING UP FOR YOU? HOW DO YOU WANT TO FEEL TODAY?

....

....

....

Day 55

SAY THIS AFFIRMATION OUT LOUD WITH YOUR HAND ON YOUR HEART:

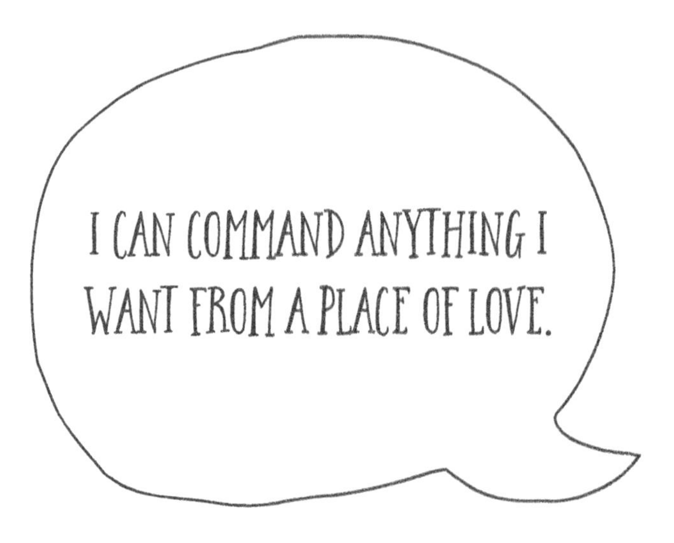

NOW WRITE IT OUT 10 TIMES:

1 ....

....

2 ....

....

3 ....

....

4 ....

....

5 ....

....

6 ....

....

7 ....

....

8 ....

....

9 ....

....

10 ....

....

NOW REPEAT THIS THREE TIMES WITH YOUR HAND ON YOUR HEART:

♥ ♥ ♥

"I'M HAPPY TO KNOW THAT I CAN COMMAND ANYTHING I WANT WHEN IT COMES FROM A PLACE OF LOVE."

♥ ♥ ♥

NOW WRITE HOW YOU FEEL AFTER COMPLETING THIS EXCERCISE. DOES IT BRING ANYTHING UP FOR YOU? HOW DO YOU WANT TO FEEL TODAY?

....

....

....

Day 56

SAY THIS AFFIRMATION OUT LOUD WITH YOUR HAND ON YOUR HEART:

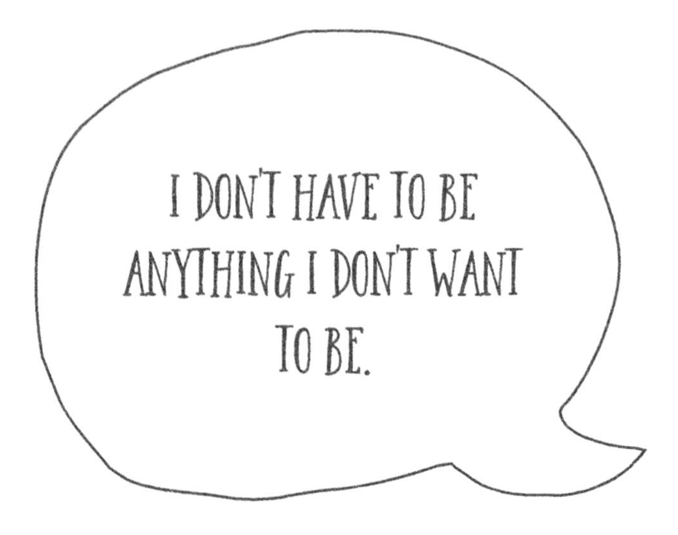

NOW WRITE IT OUT 10 TIMES:

1 ....

....

2 ....

....

3 ....

....

4 ....

....

5 ....

....

6 ....

....

7 ....

....

8 ....

....

9 ....

....

10 ....

....

NOW REPEAT THIS THREE TIMES WITH YOUR HAND ON YOUR HEART:

♥♥♥

"I'M SO HAPPY AND GRATEFUL THAT I DON'T HAVE TO BE ANYTHING I DON'T WANT TO BE."

♥♥♥

NOW WRITE HOW YOU FEEL AFTER COMPLETING THIS EXCERCISE. DOES IT BRING ANYTHING UP FOR YOU? HOW DO YOU WANT TO FEEL TODAY?

....

....

....

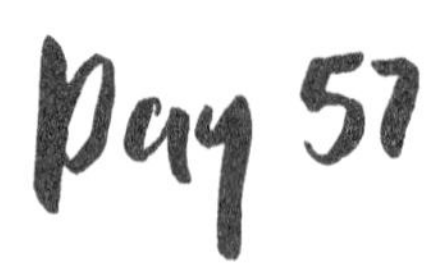

Day 57

SAY THIS AFFIRMATION OUT LOUD WITH YOUR HAND ON YOUR HEART:

NOW WRITE IT OUT 10 TIMES:

1 ....

....

2 ....

....

3 ....

....

4 ....

....

5 ....

....

6 ....

....

7 ....

....

8 ....

....

9 ....

....

10 ....

....

NOW REPEAT THIS THREE TIMES WITH YOUR HAND ON YOUR HEART:

♥♥♥

"I LOVE KNOWING THAT I AM HERE TO SERVE AND LOVE. IT GIVES ME GREAT CONFIDENCE."

♥♥♥

NOW WRITE HOW YOU FEEL AFTER COMPLETING THIS EXCERCISE. DOES IT BRING ANYTHING UP FOR YOU? HOW DO YOU WANT TO FEEL TODAY?

....

....

....

Day 58

SAY THIS AFFIRMATION OUT LOUD WITH YOUR HAND ON YOUR HEART:

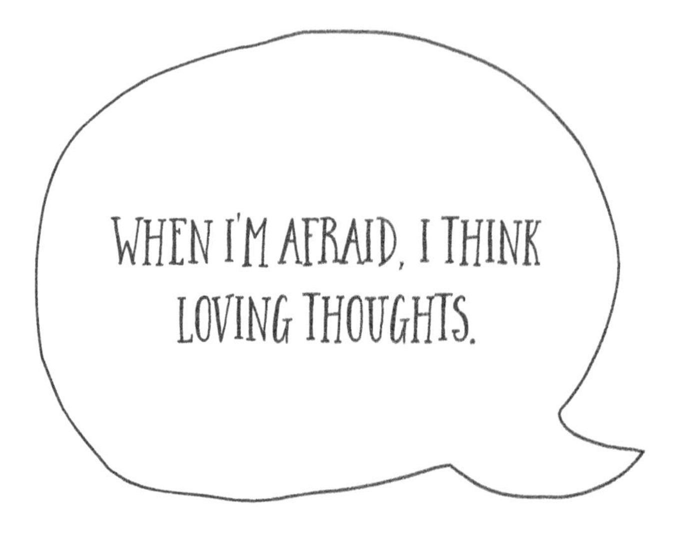

NOW WRITE IT OUT 10 TIMES:

1 ....

....

2 ....

....

3 ....

....

4 ....

....

5 ....

....

6 ....

....

7 ....

....

8 ....

....

9 ....

....

10 ....

....

NOW REPEAT THIS THREE TIMES WITH YOUR HAND ON YOUR HEART:

♥♥♥

"I'M GRATEFUL THAT LOVING THOUGHTS HELP ME TO MOVE PAST FEELINGS OF FEAR."

♥♥♥

NOW WRITE HOW YOU FEEL AFTER COMPLETING THIS EXCERCISE. DOES IT BRING ANYTHING UP FOR YOU? HOW DO YOU WANT TO FEEL TODAY?

....

....

....

Day 59

SAY THIS AFFIRMATION OUT LOUD WITH YOUR HAND ON YOUR HEART:

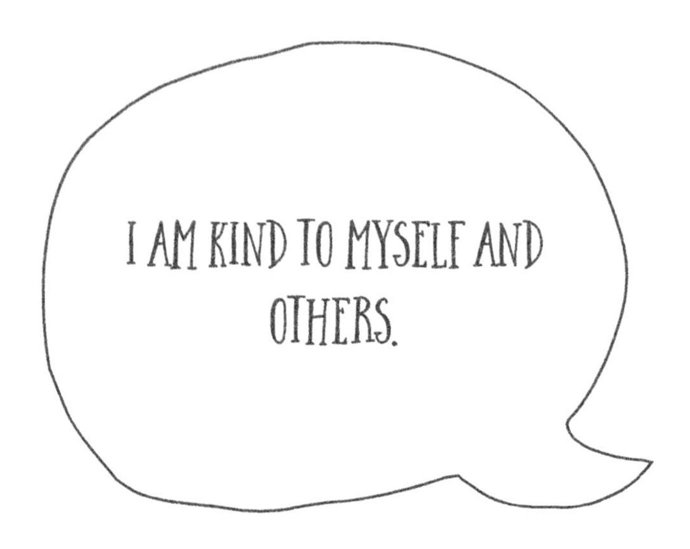

NOW WRITE IT OUT 10 TIMES:

1 ....

....

2 ....

....

3 ....

....

4 ....

....

5 ....

....

6 ....

....

7 ....

....

8 ....

....

9 ....

....

10 ....

....

NOW REPEAT THIS THREE TIMES WITH YOUR HAND ON YOUR HEART:

♥♥♥

"BEING KIND TO MYSELF AND OTHERS FILLS ME WITH GRATITUDE AND JOY."

♥♥♥

NOW WRITE HOW YOU FEEL AFTER COMPLETING THIS EXCERCISE. DOES IT BRING ANYTHING UP FOR YOU? HOW DO YOU WANT TO FEEL TODAY?

....

....

....

Day 60

SAY THIS AFFIRMATION OUT LOUD WITH YOUR HAND ON YOUR HEART:

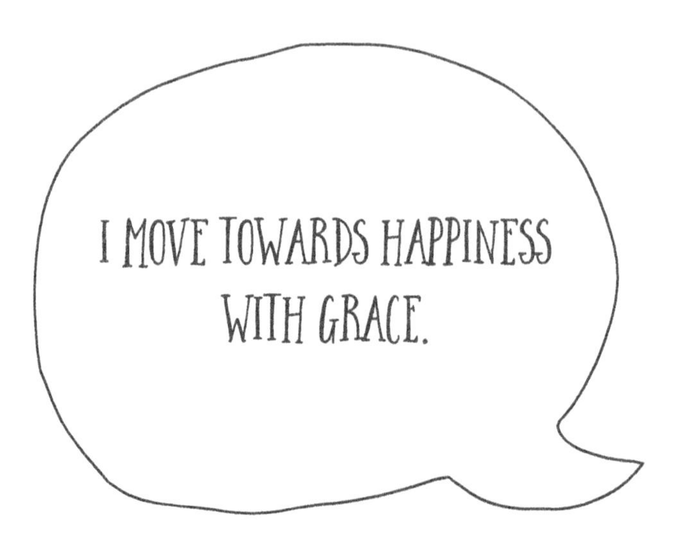

NOW WRITE IT OUT 10 TIMES:

1 ....

....

2 ....

....

3 ....

....

4 ....

....

5 ....

....

6 ....

....

7 ....

....

8 ....

....

9 ....

....

10 ....

....

NOW REPEAT THIS THREE TIMES WITH YOUR HAND ON YOUR HEART:

♥♥♥

"I SEND LOVE AND APPRECIATION TO MYSELF AS I MOVE TOWARDS HAPPINESS."

♥♥♥

NOW WRITE HOW YOU FEEL AFTER COMPLETING THIS EXCERCISE. DOES IT BRING ANYTHING UP FOR YOU? HOW DO YOU WANT TO FEEL TODAY?

....

....

....

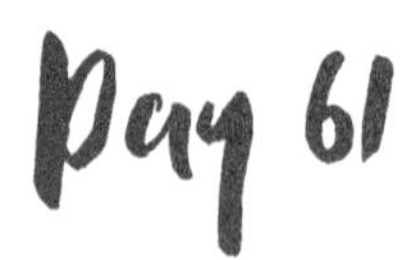

SAY THIS AFFIRMATION OUT LOUD WITH YOUR HAND ON YOUR HEART:

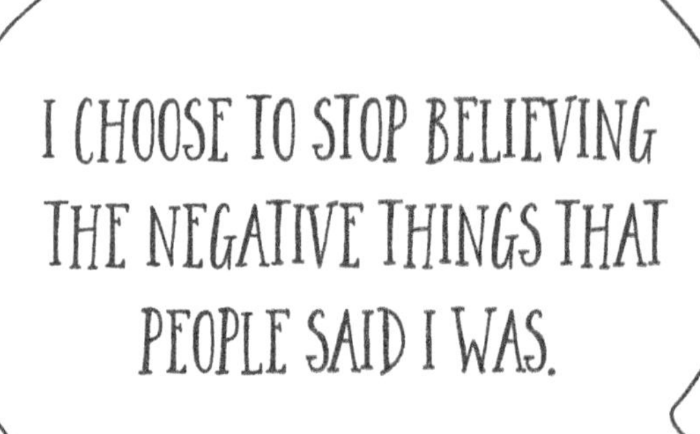

NOW WRITE IT OUT 10 TIMES:

1 ....

....

2 ....

....

3 ....

....

4 ....

....

5 ....

....

6 ....

....

7 ....

....

8 ....

....

9 ....

....

10 ....

....

NOW REPEAT THIS THREE TIMES WITH YOUR HAND ON YOUR HEART:

♥♥♥

"I'M SO HAPPY AND GRATEFUL THAT I'M FREEING MYSELF UP FROM NEGATIVE LABELS."

♥♥♥

NOW WRITE HOW YOU FEEL AFTER COMPLETING THIS EXCERCISE. DOES IT BRING ANYTHING UP FOR YOU? HOW DO YOU WANT TO FEEL TODAY?

....

....

....

Day 62

SAY THIS AFFIRMATION OUT LOUD WITH YOUR HAND ON YOUR HEART:

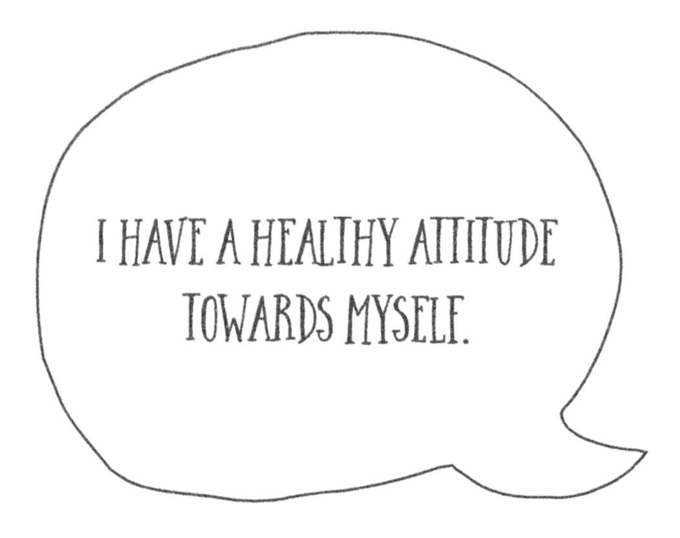

NOW WRITE IT OUT 10 TIMES:

1 ....

....

2 ....

....

3 ....

....

4 ....

....

5 ....

....

6 ....

....

7 ....

....

8 ....

....

9 ....

....

10 ....

....

NOW REPEAT THIS THREE TIMES WITH YOUR HAND ON YOUR HEART:

♥♥♥

"I APPRECIATE MY NEW, HEALTHY ATTITUDE TOWARDS MYSELF."

♥♥♥

NOW WRITE HOW YOU FEEL AFTER COMPLETING THIS EXCERCISE. DOES IT BRING ANYTHING UP FOR YOU? HOW DO YOU WANT TO FEEL TODAY?

....

....

....

SAY THIS AFFIRMATION OUT LOUD WITH YOUR HAND ON YOUR HEART:

NOW WRITE IT OUT 10 TIMES:

1 ....

....

2 ....

....

3 ....

....

4 ....

....

5 ....

....

6 ....

....

7 ....

....

8 ....

....

9 ....

....

10 ....

....

NOW REPEAT THIS THREE TIMES WITH YOUR HAND ON YOUR HEART:

♥♥♥

"I'M GRATEFUL THAT I HAVE BEEN ABLE TO CREATE THIS NEW HABIT."

♥♥♥

NOW WRITE HOW YOU FEEL AFTER COMPLETING THIS EXCERCISE. DOES IT BRING ANYTHING UP FOR YOU? HOW DO YOU WANT TO FEEL TODAY?

....

....

....

Day 64

SAY THIS AFFIRMATION OUT LOUD WITH YOUR HAND ON YOUR HEART:

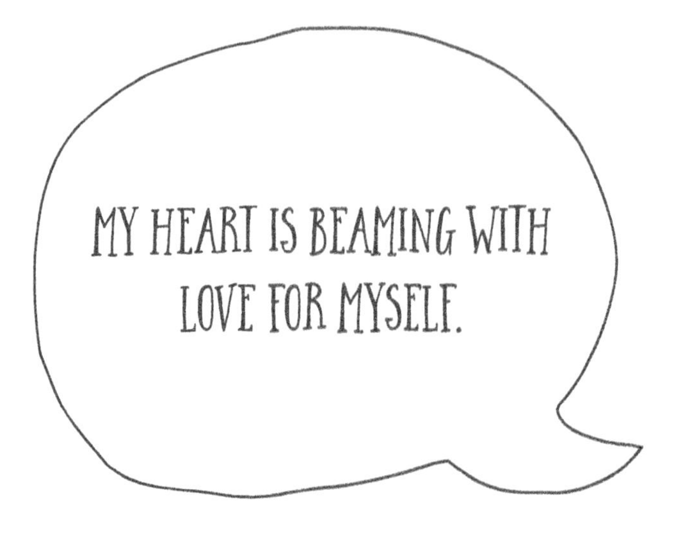

NOW WRITE IT OUT 10 TIMES:

1 ....

....

2 ....

....

3 ....

....

4 ....

....

5 ....

....

6 ....

....

7 ....

....

8 ....

....

9 ....

....

10 ....

....

NOW REPEAT THIS THREE TIMES WITH YOUR HAND ON YOUR HEART:

♥♥♥

"I'M SO HAPPY AND GRATEFUL MY HEART IS BEAMING WITH LOVE FOR MYSELF."

♥♥♥

NOW WRITE HOW YOU FEEL AFTER COMPLETING THIS EXCERCISE. DOES IT BRING ANYTHING UP FOR YOU? HOW DO YOU WANT TO FEEL TODAY?

....

....

....

Day 65

SAY THIS AFFIRMATION OUT LOUD WITH YOUR HAND ON YOUR HEART:

NOW WRITE IT OUT 10 TIMES:

1 ....

....

2 ....

....

3 ....

....

4 ....

....

5 ....

....

6 ....

....

7 ....

....

8 ....

....

9 ....

....

10 ....

....

NOW REPEAT THIS THREE TIMES WITH YOUR HAND ON YOUR HEART:

♥♥♥

"I GIVE THANKS THAT MY HEART IS BEAMING WITH LOVE FOR OTHER PEOPLE."

♥♥♥

NOW WRITE HOW YOU FEEL AFTER COMPLETING THIS EXCERCISE. DOES IT BRING ANYTHING UP FOR YOU? HOW DO YOU WANT TO FEEL TODAY?

....

....

....

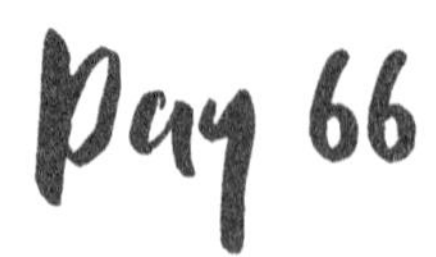

SAY THIS AFFIRMATION OUT LOUD WITH YOUR HAND ON YOUR HEART:

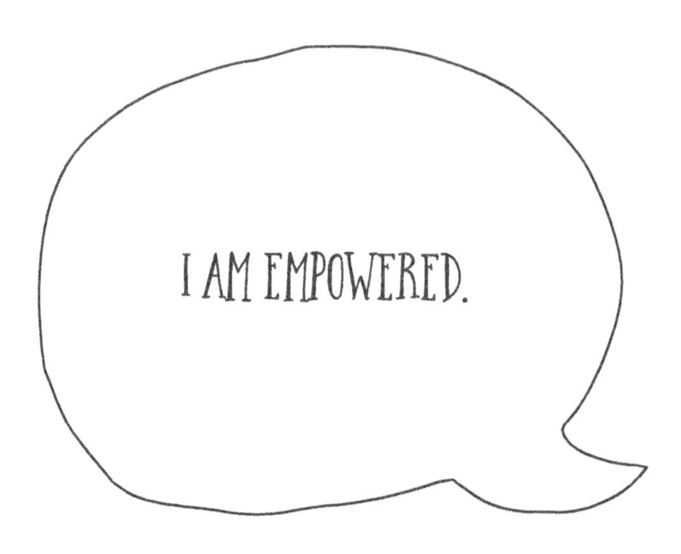

NOW WRITE IT OUT 10 TIMES:

1 ....

....

2 ....

....

3 ....

....

4 ....

....

5 ....

....

6

7

8

9

10

NOW REPEAT THIS THREE TIMES WITH YOUR HAND ON YOUR HEART:

"I'M SO HAPPY AND GRATEFUL THAT I'M NOW FEELING EMPOWERED."

NOW WRITE HOW YOU FEEL AFTER COMPLETING THIS EXCERCISE. DOES IT BRING ANYTHING UP FOR YOU? HOW DO YOU WANT TO FEEL TODAY?

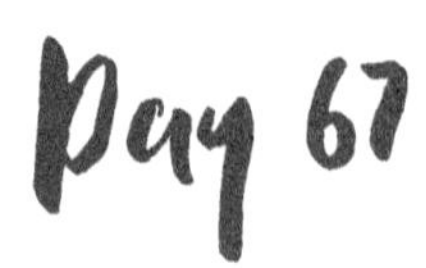

SAY THIS AFFIRMATION OUT LOUD WITH YOUR HAND ON YOUR HEART:

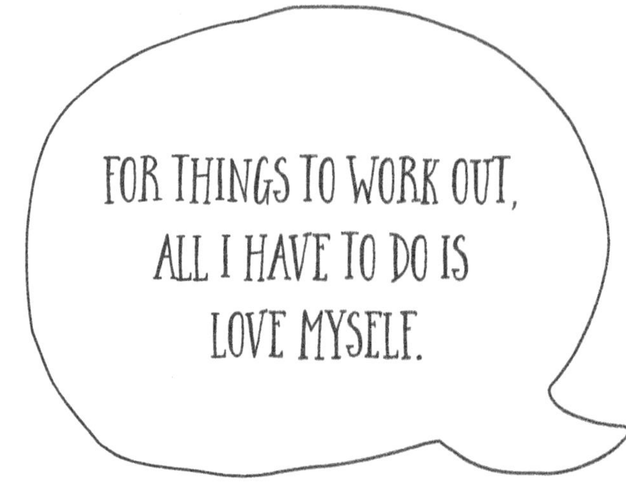

NOW WRITE IT OUT 10 TIMES:

1 ....

....

2 ....

....

3 ....

....

4 ....

....

5 ....

....

6 ....

....

7 ....

....

8 ....

....

9 ....

....

10 ....

....

NOW REPEAT THIS THREE TIMES WITH YOUR HAND ON YOUR HEART:

♥♥♥

"I ALWAYS EXPRESS THE DEEPEST LOVE FOR MYSELF AND APPRECIATE THE WAY THAT FEELS."

♥♥♥

NOW WRITE HOW YOU FEEL AFTER COMPLETING THIS EXCERCISE. DOES IT BRING ANYTHING UP FOR YOU? HOW DO YOU WANT TO FEEL TODAY?

....

....

....

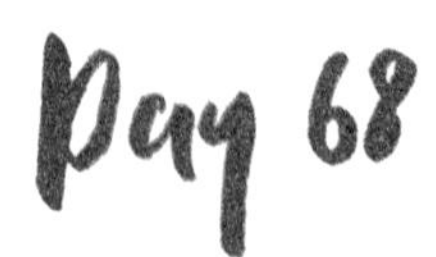

SAY THIS AFFIRMATION OUT LOUD WITH YOUR HAND ON YOUR HEART:

NOW WRITE IT OUT 10 TIMES:

1 ....

....

2 ....

....

3 ....

....

4 ....

....

5 ....

....

6 ....

....

7 ....

....

8 ....

....

9 ....

....

10 ....

....

NOW REPEAT THIS THREE TIMES WITH YOUR HAND ON YOUR HEART:

♥♥♥

"I APPRECIATE THE NEW CONFIDENCE WITHIN MYSELF THAT I HAVE FOUND AND LET IT EXPAND."

♥♥♥

NOW WRITE HOW YOU FEEL AFTER COMPLETING THIS EXCERCISE. DOES IT BRING ANYTHING UP FOR YOU? HOW DO YOU WANT TO FEEL TODAY?

....

....

....

SAY THIS AFFIRMATION OUT LOUD WITH YOUR HAND ON YOUR HEART:

NOW WRITE IT OUT 10 TIMES:

1 ....

....

2 ....

....

3 ....

....

4 ....

....

5 ....

....

6 ....

....

7 ....

....

8 ....

....

9 ....

....

10 ....

....

NOW REPEAT THIS THREE TIMES WITH YOUR HAND ON YOUR HEART:

"I'M SO GRATEFUL THAT MY NEW, IMPROVED OUTLOOK IS MAKING ME FEEL HAPPY."

NOW WRITE HOW YOU FEEL AFTER COMPLETING THIS EXCERCISE. DOES IT BRING ANYTHING UP FOR YOU? HOW DO YOU WANT TO FEEL TODAY?

....

....

....

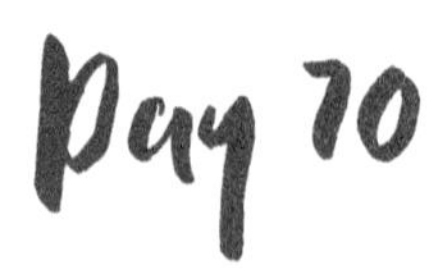

SAY THIS AFFIRMATION OUT LOUD WITH YOUR HAND ON YOUR HEART:

NOW WRITE IT OUT 10 TIMES:

1 ....

....

2 ....

....

3 ....

....

4 ....

....

5 ....

....

6 ....

....

7 ....

....

8 ....

....

9 ....

....

10 ....

....

NOW REPEAT THIS THREE TIMES WITH YOUR HAND ON YOUR HEART:

"I'M GRATEFUL MY CONFIDENCE IS GROWING DAILY AND I FEEL GOOD ABOUT MYSELF."

NOW WRITE HOW YOU FEEL AFTER COMPLETING THIS EXCERCISE. DOES IT BRING ANYTHING UP FOR YOU? HOW DO YOU WANT TO FEEL TODAY?

....

....

....

SAY THIS AFFIRMATION OUT LOUD WITH YOUR HAND ON YOUR HEART:

NOW WRITE IT OUT 10 TIMES:

1 ....

....

2 ....

....

3 ....

....

4 ....

....

5 ....

....

6 ....

....

7 ....

....

8 ....

....

9 ....

....

10 ....

....

NOW REPEAT THIS THREE TIMES WITH YOUR HAND ON YOUR HEART:

♥♥♥

"I APPRECIATE THE CHANGES I MAKE TO IMPROVE MY SELF-LOVE AND CONFIDENCE."

♥♥♥

NOW WRITE HOW YOU FEEL AFTER COMPLETING THIS EXCERCISE. DOES IT BRING ANYTHING UP FOR YOU? HOW DO YOU WANT TO FEEL TODAY?

....

....

....

SAY THIS AFFIRMATION OUT LOUD WITH YOUR HAND ON YOUR HEART:

NOW WRITE IT OUT 10 TIMES:

1 ....

....

2 ....

....

3 ....

....

4 ....

....

5 ....

....

6 ....

....

7 ....

....

8 ....

....

9 ....

....

10 ....

....

NOW REPEAT THIS THREE TIMES WITH YOUR HAND ON YOUR HEART:

"I'M SO HAPPY AND GRATEFUL THAT LOVE IS AVAILABLE TO ME AND FREE OF RESISTANCE."

NOW WRITE HOW YOU FEEL AFTER COMPLETING THIS EXCERCISE. DOES IT BRING ANYTHING UP FOR YOU? HOW DO YOU WANT TO FEEL TODAY?

....

....

....

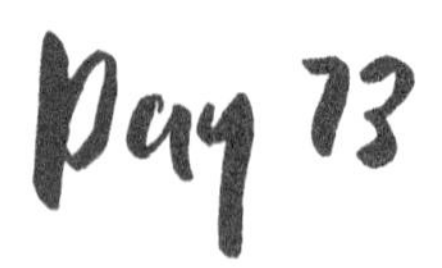

SAY THIS AFFIRMATION OUT LOUD WITH YOUR HAND ON YOUR HEART:

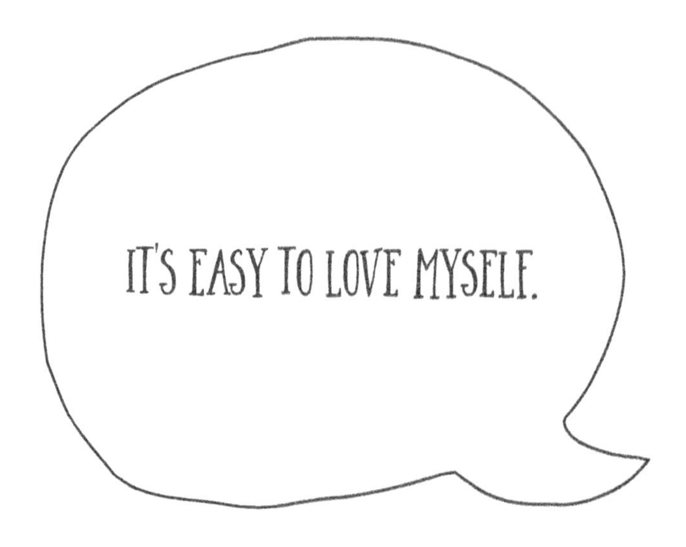

NOW WRITE IT OUT 10 TIMES:

1 ....

....

2 ....

....

3 ....

....

4 ....

....

5 ....

....

6 ....

....

7 ....

....

8 ....

....

9 ....

....

10 ....

....

NOW REPEAT THIS THREE TIMES WITH YOUR HAND ON YOUR HEART:

"I'M SO HAPPY AND GRATEFUL THAT LOVING MYSELF IS AN EASY THING TO DO."

NOW WRITE HOW YOU FEEL AFTER COMPLETING THIS EXCERCISE. DOES IT BRING ANYTHING UP FOR YOU? HOW DO YOU WANT TO FEEL TODAY?

....

....

....

SAY THIS AFFIRMATION OUT LOUD WITH YOUR HAND ON YOUR HEART:

NOW WRITE IT OUT 10 TIMES:

1 ....

....

2 ....

....

3 ....

....

4 ....

....

5 ....

....

6 ....

....

7 ....

....

8 ....

....

9 ....

....

10 ....

....

NOW REPEAT THIS THREE TIMES WITH YOUR HAND ON YOUR HEART:

♥♥♥

"I NOW REALISE THAT I'M WORTHY OF LOVE
AND FOR THIS I AM VERY GRATEFUL."

NOW WRITE HOW YOU FEEL AFTER COMPLETING THIS EXCERCISE. DOES IT BRING ANYTHING UP FOR YOU? HOW DO YOU WANT TO FEEL TODAY?

....

....

....

SAY THIS AFFIRMATION OUT LOUD WITH YOUR HAND ON YOUR HEART:

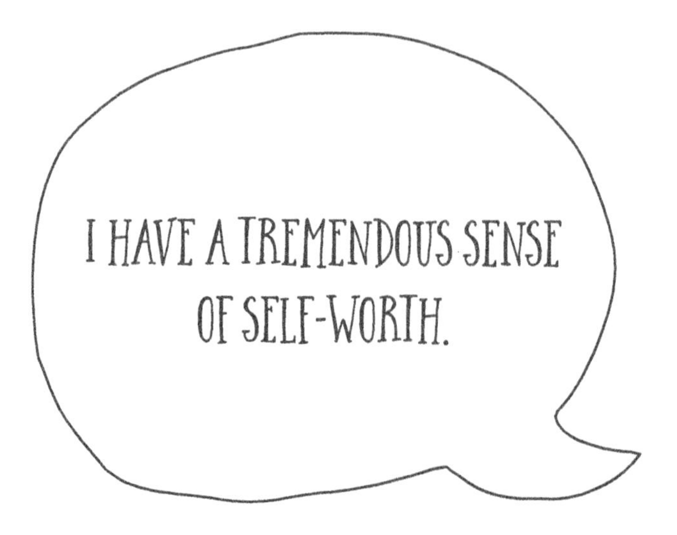

NOW WRITE IT OUT 10 TIMES:

1 ....

....

2 ....

....

3 ....

....

4 ....

....

5 ....

....

6 ....

....

7 ....

....

8 ....

....

9 ....

....

10 ....

....

NOW REPEAT THIS THREE TIMES WITH YOUR HAND ON YOUR HEART:

♥♥♥

"SELF-WORTH IS A POSITIVE THING TO HAVE AND I'M GRATEFUL I CAN ACCESS THAT NOW."

♥♥♥

NOW WRITE HOW YOU FEEL AFTER COMPLETING THIS EXCERCISE. DOES IT BRING ANYTHING UP FOR YOU? HOW DO YOU WANT TO FEEL TODAY?

....

....

....

SAY THIS AFFIRMATION OUT LOUD WITH YOUR HAND ON YOUR HEART:

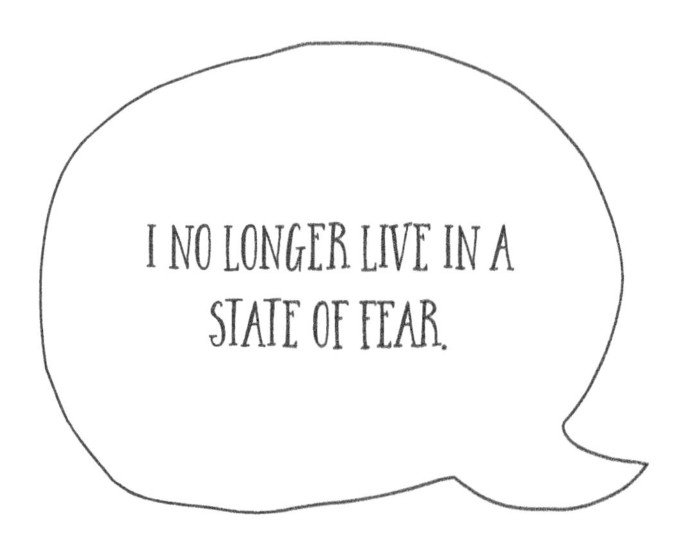

NOW WRITE IT OUT 10 TIMES:

1 ....

....

2 ....

....

3 ....

....

4 ....

....

5 ....

....

6

7

8

9

10

NOW REPEAT THIS THREE TIMES WITH YOUR HAND ON YOUR HEART:

"I'M SO HAPPY AND GRATEFUL THAT I'M FREE FROM FEAR."

NOW WRITE HOW YOU FEEL AFTER COMPLETING THIS EXCERCISE. DOES IT BRING ANYTHING UP FOR YOU? HOW DO YOU WANT TO FEEL TODAY?

SAY THIS AFFIRMATION OUT LOUD WITH YOUR HAND ON YOUR HEART:

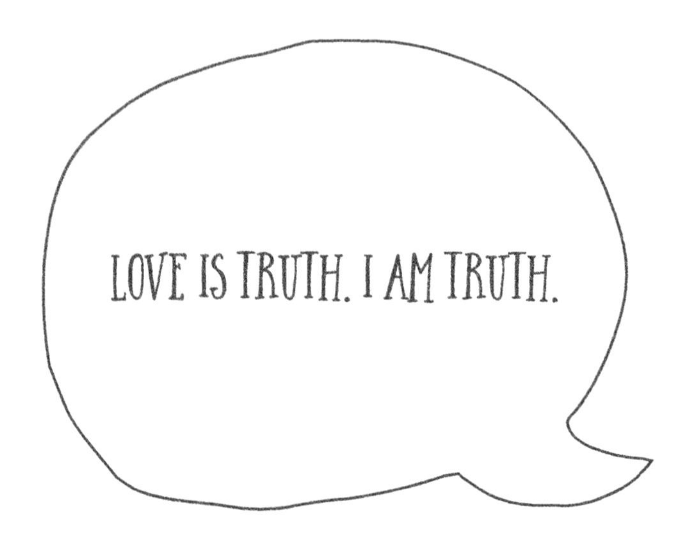

NOW WRITE IT OUT 10 TIMES:

1 ....

....

2 ....

....

3 ....

....

4 ....

....

5 ....

....

6 ....

....

7 ....

....

8 ....

....

9 ....

....

10 ....

....

NOW REPEAT THIS THREE TIMES WITH YOUR HAND ON YOUR HEART:

♥♥♥

"I NOTICE AND APPRECIATE ALL THE LOVE PRESENT IN THE WORLD."

♥♥♥

NOW WRITE HOW YOU FEEL AFTER COMPLETING THIS EXCERCISE. DOES IT BRING ANYTHING UP FOR YOU? HOW DO YOU WANT TO FEEL TODAY?

....

....

....

Day 78

SAY THIS AFFIRMATION OUT LOUD WITH YOUR HAND ON YOUR HEART:

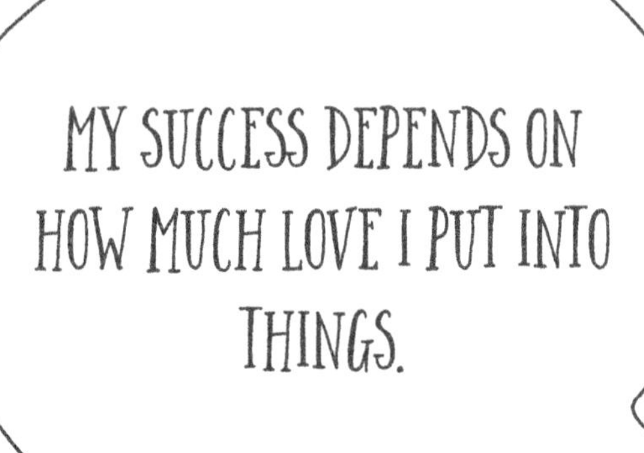

NOW WRITE IT OUT 10 TIMES:

1 ....

....

2 ....

....

3 ....

....

4 ....

....

5 ....

....

6 ....

....

7 ....

....

8 ....

....

9 ....

....

10 ....

....

NOW REPEAT THIS THREE TIMES WITH YOUR HAND ON YOUR HEART:

♥♥♥

"I APPRECIATE THAT THE BIGGEST SUCCESS IN LIFE IS TO SHARE LOVE AND BE LOVE."

♥♥♥

NOW WRITE HOW YOU FEEL AFTER COMPLETING THIS EXCERCISE. DOES IT BRING ANYTHING UP FOR YOU? HOW DO YOU WANT TO FEEL TODAY?

....

....

....

SAY THIS AFFIRMATION OUT LOUD WITH YOUR HAND ON YOUR HEART:

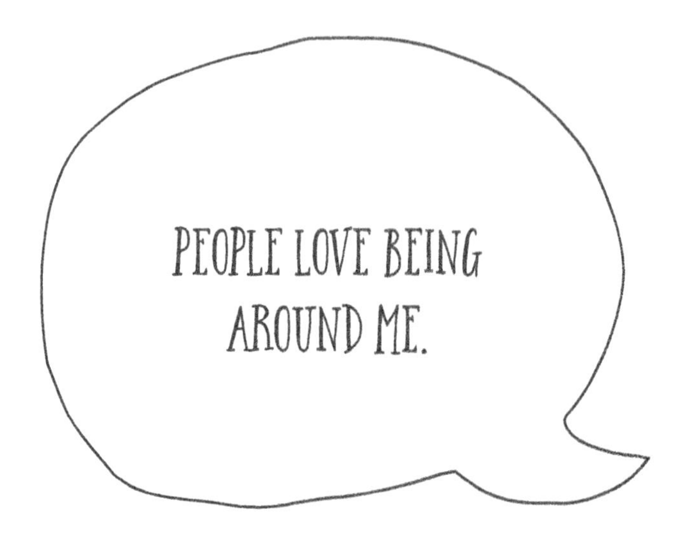

NOW WRITE IT OUT 10 TIMES:

1 ....

....

2 ....

....

3 ....

....

4 ....

....

5 ....

....

6 ....

7 ....

8 ....

9 ....

10 ....

NOW REPEAT THIS THREE TIMES WITH YOUR HAND ON YOUR HEART:

♥♥♥

"I GIVE THANKS THAT OTHER PEOPLE LOVE BEING AROUND ME AND SEE MY GOOD QUALITIES."

♥♥♥

NOW WRITE HOW YOU FEEL AFTER COMPLETING THIS EXCERCISE. DOES IT BRING ANYTHING UP FOR YOU? HOW DO YOU WANT TO FEEL TODAY?

....

....

....

Day 80

SAY THIS AFFIRMATION OUT LOUD WITH YOUR HAND ON YOUR HEART:

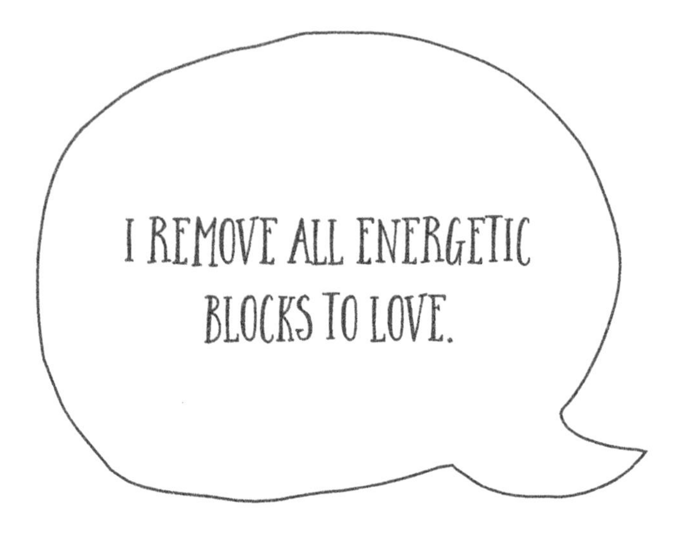

NOW WRITE IT OUT 10 TIMES:

1 ....

....

2 ....

....

3 ....

....

4 ....

....

5 ....

....

6 ....

....

7 ....

....

8 ....

....

9 ....

....

10 ....

....

NOW REPEAT THIS THREE TIMES WITH YOUR HAND ON YOUR HEART:

♥♥♥

"I'M SO HAPPY AND GRATEFUL THAT I'M REMOVING ANY ENERGETIC BLOCKS TO LOVE."

♥♥♥

NOW WRITE HOW YOU FEEL AFTER COMPLETING THIS EXCERCISE. DOES IT BRING ANYTHING UP FOR YOU? HOW DO YOU WANT TO FEEL TODAY?

....

....

....

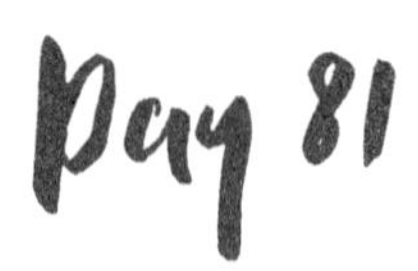

SAY THIS AFFIRMATION OUT LOUD WITH YOUR HAND ON YOUR HEART:

NOW WRITE IT OUT 10 TIMES:

1 ....

....

2 ....

....

3 ....

....

4 ....

....

5 ....

....

6 ....

....

7 ....

....

8 ....

....

9 ....

....

10 ....

....

NOW REPEAT THIS THREE TIMES WITH YOUR HAND ON YOUR HEART:

♥♥♥

"I APPRECIATE THE FEELING OF LOVE RUNNING THROUGH MY VEINS. IT IS REAL."

♥♥♥

NOW WRITE HOW YOU FEEL AFTER COMPLETING THIS EXCERCISE. DOES IT BRING ANYTHING UP FOR YOU? HOW DO YOU WANT TO FEEL TODAY?

....

....

....

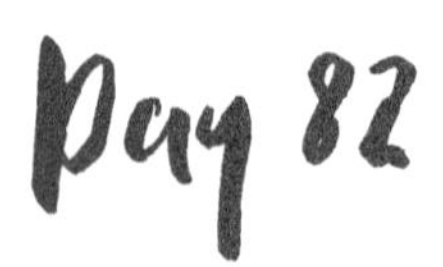

SAY THIS AFFIRMATION OUT LOUD WITH YOUR HAND ON YOUR HEART:

NOW WRITE IT OUT 10 TIMES:

1 ....

....

2 ....

....

3 ....

....

4 ....

....

5 ....

....

6 ....

....

7 ....

....

8 ....

....

9 ....

....

10 ....

....

NOW REPEAT THIS THREE TIMES WITH YOUR HAND ON YOUR HEART:

♥♥♥

"I LOVE THE FREEDOM THAT COMES FROM THE REALISATION THAT I DON'T NEED OTHER'S APPROVAL."

♥♥♥

NOW WRITE HOW YOU FEEL AFTER COMPLETING THIS EXCERCISE. DOES IT BRING ANYTHING UP FOR YOU? HOW DO YOU WANT TO FEEL TODAY?

....

....

....

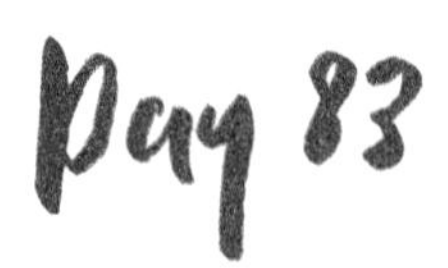

SAY THIS AFFIRMATION OUT LOUD WITH YOUR HAND ON YOUR HEART:

NOW WRITE IT OUT 10 TIMES:

1 ....

....

2 ....

....

3 ....

....

4 ....

....

5 ....

....

6

7

8

9

10

NOW REPEAT THIS THREE TIMES WITH YOUR HAND ON YOUR HEART:

"I'M SO HAPPY AND GRATEFUL THAT I GIVE MYSELF PERMISSION TO LOVE MYSELF."

NOW WRITE HOW YOU FEEL AFTER COMPLETING THIS EXCERCISE. DOES IT BRING ANYTHING UP FOR YOU? HOW DO YOU WANT TO FEEL TODAY?

SAY THIS AFFIRMATION OUT LOUD WITH YOUR HAND ON YOUR HEART:

NOW WRITE IT OUT 10 TIMES:

1 ....

....

2 ....

....

3 ....

....

4 ....

....

5 ....

....

6 ....

....

7 ....

....

8 ....

....

9 ....

....

10 ....

....

NOW REPEAT THIS THREE TIMES WITH YOUR HAND ON YOUR HEART:

♥♥♥

"I SEND LOVE TO WHO I REALLY AM. I UNDERSTAND THAT NOBODY KNOWS ME LIKE I KNOW ME."

♥♥♥

NOW WRITE HOW YOU FEEL AFTER COMPLETING THIS EXCERCISE. DOES IT BRING ANYTHING UP FOR YOU? HOW DO YOU WANT TO FEEL TODAY?

....

....

....

SAY THIS AFFIRMATION OUT LOUD WITH YOUR HAND ON YOUR HEART:

NOW WRITE IT OUT 10 TIMES:

1 ....

....

2 ....

....

3 ....

....

4 ....

....

5 ....

....

6 ....

....

7 ....

....

8 ....

....

9 ....

....

10 ....

....

NOW REPEAT THIS THREE TIMES WITH YOUR HAND ON YOUR HEART:

♥♥♥

"I'M GRATEFUL THAT SELF-LOVE AND CONFIDENCE IS AVAILABLE TO ME NOW."

♥♥♥

NOW WRITE HOW YOU FEEL AFTER COMPLETING THIS EXCERCISE. DOES IT BRING ANYTHING UP FOR YOU? HOW DO YOU WANT TO FEEL TODAY?

....

....

....

Day 86

SAY THIS AFFIRMATION OUT LOUD WITH YOUR HAND ON YOUR HEART:

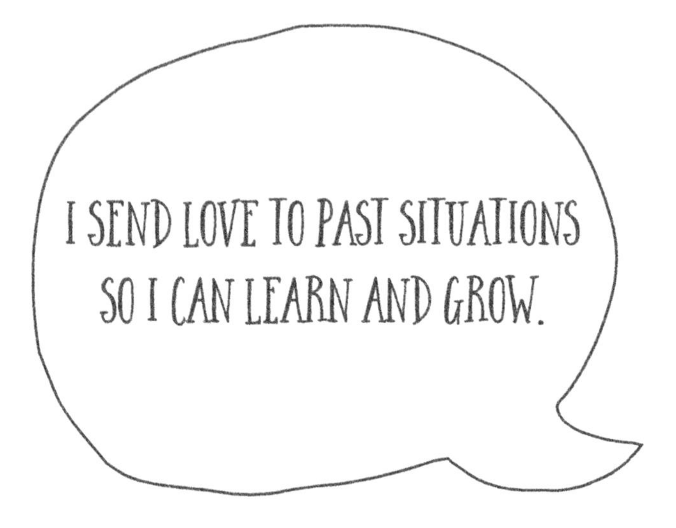

NOW WRITE IT OUT 10 TIMES:

1 ....

....

2 ....

....

3 ....

....

4 ....

....

5 ....

....

6 ....

....

7 ....

....

8 ....

....

9 ....

....

10 ....

....

NOW REPEAT THIS THREE TIMES WITH YOUR HAND ON YOUR HEART:

♥♥♥

"I'M SO HAPPY AND GRATEFUL TO LEAVE THE PAST BEHIND. I MOVE FORWARD WITH NEW KNOWLEDGE."

♥♥♥

NOW WRITE HOW YOU FEEL AFTER COMPLETING THIS EXCERCISE. DOES IT BRING ANYTHING UP FOR YOU? HOW DO YOU WANT TO FEEL TODAY?

....

....

....

SAY THIS AFFIRMATION OUT LOUD WITH YOUR HAND ON YOUR HEART:

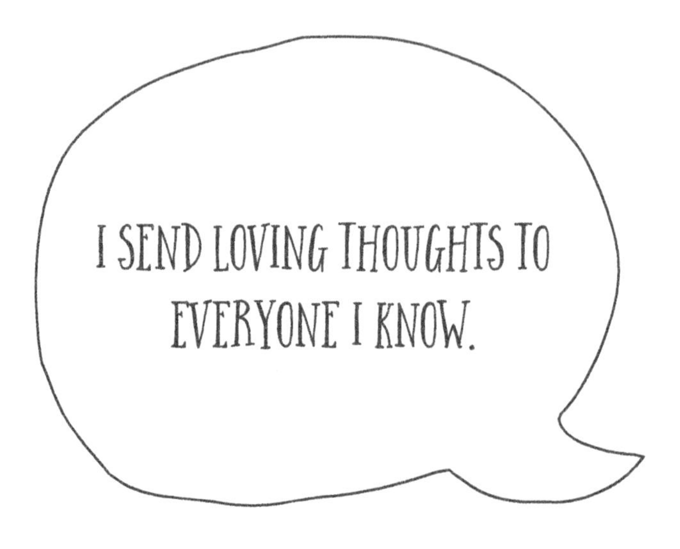

NOW WRITE IT OUT 10 TIMES:

1 ....

....

2 ....

....

3 ....

....

4 ....

....

5 ....

....

6 ....

....

7 ....

....

8 ....

....

9 ....

....

10 ....

....

NOW REPEAT THIS THREE TIMES WITH YOUR HAND ON YOUR HEART:

♥♥♥

"I'M SO HAPPY AND GRATEFUL THAT SENDING LOVING THOUGHTS OUT MAKES ME FEEL SO GOOD."

♥♥♥

NOW WRITE HOW YOU FEEL AFTER COMPLETING THIS EXCERCISE. DOES IT BRING ANYTHING UP FOR YOU? HOW DO YOU WANT TO FEEL TODAY?

....

....

....

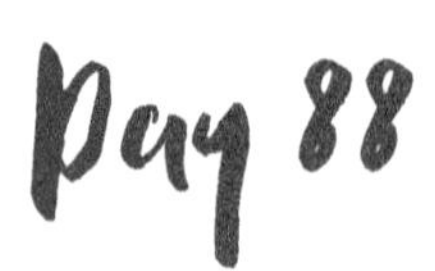

SAY THIS AFFIRMATION OUT LOUD WITH YOUR HAND ON YOUR HEART:

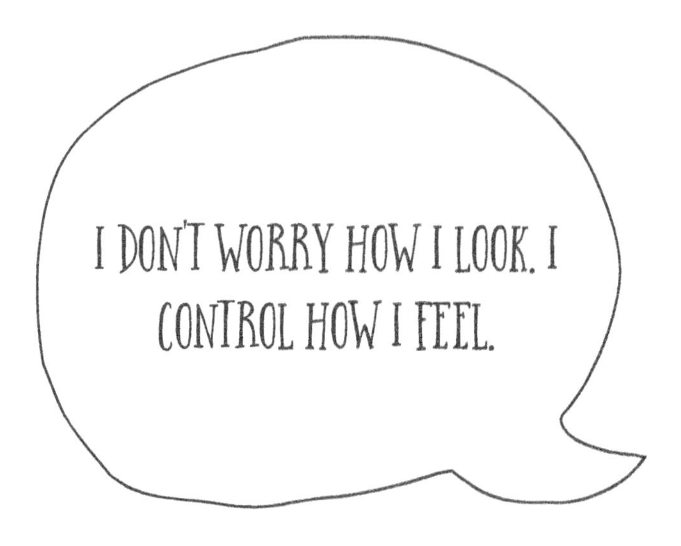

NOW WRITE IT OUT 10 TIMES:

1 ....

....

2 ....

....

3 ....

....

4 ....

....

5 ....

....

6 ....

....

7 ....

....

8 ....

....

9 ....

....

10 ....

....

NOW REPEAT THIS THREE TIMES WITH YOUR HAND ON YOUR HEART:

♥♥♥

"I FOCUS MY GRATITUDE ON MY BODY TODAY. I'M THANKFUL FOR THE WAY I AM."

♥♥♥

NOW WRITE HOW YOU FEEL AFTER COMPLETING THIS EXCERCISE. DOES IT BRING ANYTHING UP FOR YOU? HOW DO YOU WANT TO FEEL TODAY?

....

....

....

SAY THIS AFFIRMATION OUT LOUD WITH YOUR HAND ON YOUR HEART:

NOW WRITE IT OUT 10 TIMES:

1 ....

....

2 ....

....

3 ....

....

4 ....

....

5 ....

....

6 ....

....

7 ....

....

8 ....

....

9 ....

....

10 ....

....

NOW REPEAT THIS THREE TIMES WITH YOUR HAND ON YOUR HEART:

♥♥♥

"I LOVE FOCUSSING ON NEW THINGS AND MOVING FORWARD WITH EASE."

♥♥♥

NOW WRITE HOW YOU FEEL AFTER COMPLETING THIS EXCERCISE. DOES IT BRING ANYTHING UP FOR YOU? HOW DO YOU WANT TO FEEL TODAY?

....

....

....

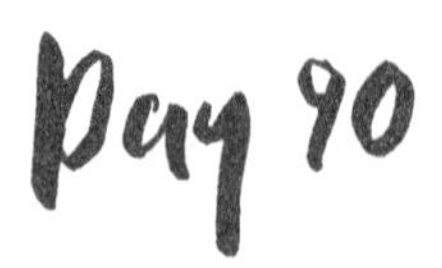

SAY THIS AFFIRMATION OUT LOUD WITH YOUR HAND ON YOUR HEART:

NOW WRITE IT OUT 10 TIMES:

1 ....

....

2 ....

....

3 ....

....

4 ....

....

5 ....

....

6

7

8

9

10

NOW REPEAT THIS THREE TIMES WITH YOUR HAND ON YOUR HEART:

"I'M SO HAPPY AND GRATEFUL MY
SELF-DOUBT IS DIMINISHING."

NOW WRITE HOW YOU FEEL AFTER COMPLETING THIS EXCERCISE. DOES IT BRING ANYTHING UP FOR YOU? HOW DO YOU WANT TO FEEL TODAY?

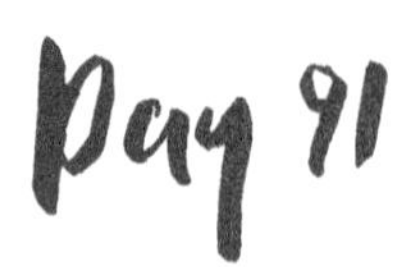

SAY THIS AFFIRMATION OUT LOUD WITH YOUR HAND ON YOUR HEART:

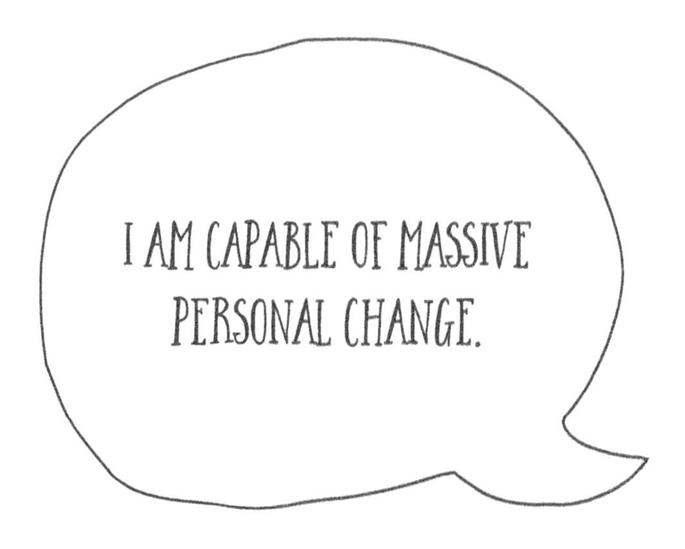

NOW WRITE IT OUT 10 TIMES:

1 ....

....

2 ....

....

3 ....

....

4 ....

....

5 ....

....

6 ....

....

7 ....

....

8 ....

....

9 ....

....

10 ....

....

NOW REPEAT THIS THREE TIMES WITH YOUR HAND ON YOUR HEART:

♥♥♥

"I DEEPLY APPRECIATE THE POSITIVE PERSONAL CHANGES I AM MAKING."

♥♥♥

NOW WRITE HOW YOU FEEL AFTER COMPLETING THIS EXCERCISE. DOES IT BRING ANYTHING UP FOR YOU? HOW DO YOU WANT TO FEEL TODAY?

....

....

....

SAY THIS AFFIRMATION OUT LOUD WITH YOUR HAND ON YOUR HEART:

NOW WRITE IT OUT 10 TIMES:

1 ....

....

2 ....

....

3 ....

....

4 ....

....

5 ....

....

6 ....

....

7 ....

....

8 ....

....

9 ....

....

10 ....

....

NOW REPEAT THIS THREE TIMES WITH YOUR HAND ON YOUR HEART:

♥♥♥

"I'M SO HAPPY AND GRATEFUL NOW THAT I'M AWARE OF MY VERY OWN PERSONAL POWER."

♥♥♥

NOW WRITE HOW YOU FEEL AFTER COMPLETING THIS EXCERCISE. DOES IT BRING ANYTHING UP FOR YOU? HOW DO YOU WANT TO FEEL TODAY?

....

....

....

Day 93

SAY THIS AFFIRMATION OUT LOUD WITH YOUR HAND ON YOUR HEART:

NOW WRITE IT OUT 10 TIMES:

1 ....

....

2 ....

....

3 ....

....

4 ....

....

5 ....

....

6 ....

....

7 ....

....

8 ....

....

9 ....

....

10 ....

....

NOW REPEAT THIS THREE TIMES WITH YOUR HAND ON YOUR HEART:

♥♥♥

"I'M SO GRATEFUL THAT I AM LEARNING TO LOVE MYSELF AND SEE EXAMPLES OF LOVE EVERYWHERE."

♥♥♥

NOW WRITE HOW YOU FEEL AFTER COMPLETING THIS EXCERCISE. DOES IT BRING ANYTHING UP FOR YOU? HOW DO YOU WANT TO FEEL TODAY?

....

....

....

SAY THIS AFFIRMATION OUT LOUD WITH YOUR HAND ON YOUR HEART:

NOW WRITE IT OUT 10 TIMES:

1 ....

....

2 ....

....

3 ....

....

4 ....

....

5 ....

....

6 ....

....

7 ....

....

8 ....

....

9 ....

....

10 ....

....

NOW REPEAT THIS THREE TIMES WITH YOUR HAND ON YOUR HEART:

♥♥♥

"I'M SO GRATEFUL THAT I'M NO LONGER BOTHERED BY OTHER PEOPLE'S WORDS. THEY HOLD NO POWER."

♥♥♥

NOW WRITE HOW YOU FEEL AFTER COMPLETING THIS EXCERCISE. DOES IT BRING ANYTHING UP FOR YOU? HOW DO YOU WANT TO FEEL TODAY?

....

....

....

Day 95

SAY THIS AFFIRMATION OUT LOUD WITH YOUR HAND ON YOUR HEART:

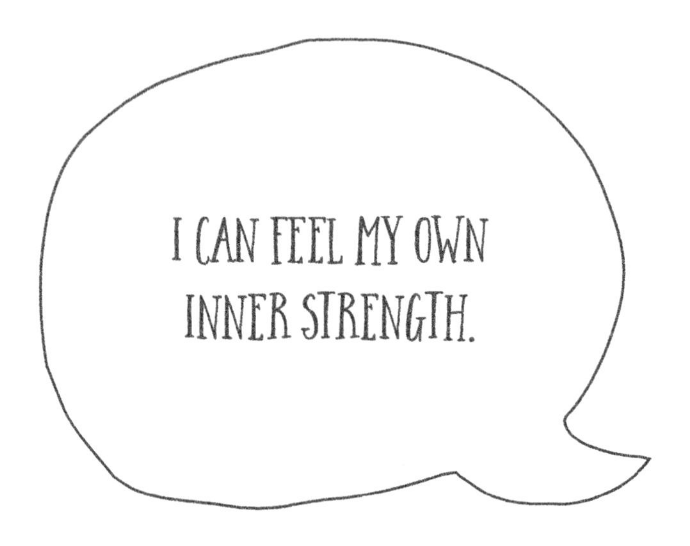

NOW WRITE IT OUT 10 TIMES:

1 ....

....

2 ....

....

3 ....

....

4 ....

....

5 ....

....

6 ....

....

7 ....

....

8 ....

....

9 ....

....

10 ....

....

NOW REPEAT THIS THREE TIMES WITH YOUR HAND ON YOUR HEART:

♥♥♥

"I'M SO HAPPY AND GRATEFUL THAT I CAN FEEL MY OWN INNER STRENGTH AND USE IT WHEN I NEED IT."

♥♥♥

NOW WRITE HOW YOU FEEL AFTER COMPLETING THIS EXCERCISE. DOES IT BRING ANYTHING UP FOR YOU? HOW DO YOU WANT TO FEEL TODAY?

....

....

....

Day 96

SAY THIS AFFIRMATION OUT LOUD WITH YOUR HAND ON YOUR HEART:

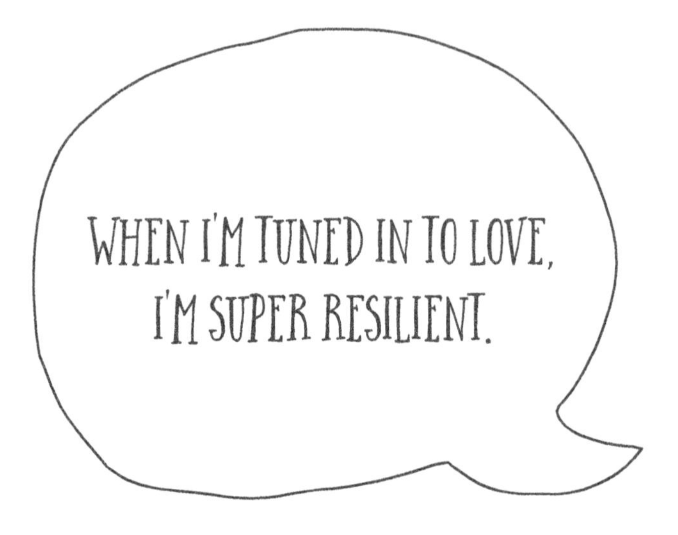

NOW WRITE IT OUT 10 TIMES:

1 ....

....

2 ....

....

3 ....

....

4 ....

....

5 ....

....

6 ....

....

7 ....

....

8 ....

....

9 ....

....

10 ....

....

NOW REPEAT THIS THREE TIMES WITH YOUR HAND ON YOUR HEART:

"I LOVE TUNING IN TO THE
FEELING OF LOVE."

NOW WRITE HOW YOU FEEL AFTER COMPLETING THIS EXCERCISE. DOES IT BRING ANYTHING UP FOR YOU? HOW DO YOU WANT TO FEEL TODAY?

....

....

....

SAY THIS AFFIRMATION OUT LOUD WITH YOUR HAND ON YOUR HEART:

NOW WRITE IT OUT 10 TIMES:

1 ....

....

2 ....

....

3 ....

....

4 ....

....

5 ....

....

6 ....

....

7 ....

....

8 ....

....

9 ....

....

10 ....

....

NOW REPEAT THIS THREE TIMES WITH YOUR HAND ON YOUR HEART:

♥♥♥

"MY CHOICE TO BOUNCE BACK AND LOVE MYSELF IS SERVING ME WELL AND I GIVE THANKS."

♥♥♥

NOW WRITE HOW YOU FEEL AFTER COMPLETING THIS EXCERCISE. DOES IT BRING ANYTHING UP FOR YOU? HOW DO YOU WANT TO FEEL TODAY?

....

....

....

Day 98

SAY THIS AFFIRMATION OUT LOUD WITH YOUR HAND ON YOUR HEART:

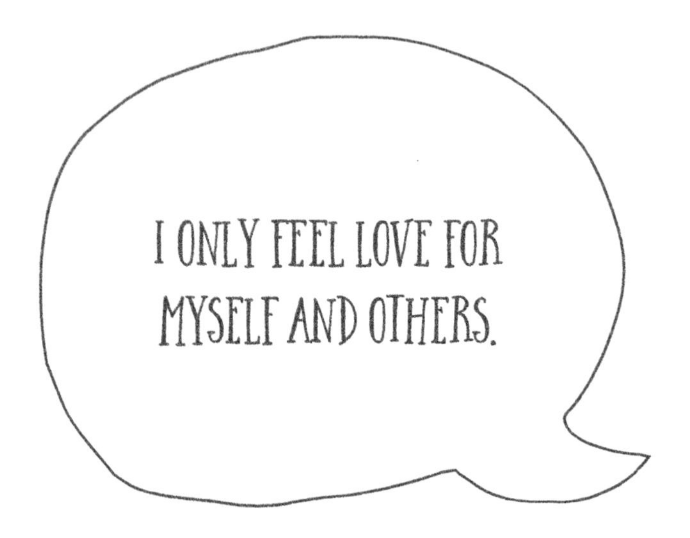

NOW WRITE IT OUT 10 TIMES:

1 ....

....

2 ....

....

3 ....

....

4 ....

....

5 ....

....

6 ....

....

7 ....

....

8 ....

....

9 ....

....

10 ....

....

NOW REPEAT THIS THREE TIMES WITH YOUR HAND ON YOUR HEART:

♥♥♥

"I'M SO HAPPY AND GRATEFUL MY NEW LOVING PERSPECTIVE FEELS REALLY GOOD."

♥♥♥

NOW WRITE HOW YOU FEEL AFTER COMPLETING THIS EXCERCISE. DOES IT BRING ANYTHING UP FOR YOU? HOW DO YOU WANT TO FEEL TODAY?

....

....

....

SAY THIS AFFIRMATION OUT LOUD WITH YOUR HAND ON YOUR HEART:

NOW WRITE IT OUT 10 TIMES:

1 ....

....

2 ....

....

3 ....

....

4 ....

....

5 ....

....

6 ....

....

7 ....

....

8 ....

....

9 ....

....

10 ....

....

NOW REPEAT THIS THREE TIMES WITH YOUR HAND ON YOUR HEART:

♥♥♥

"I'M SO HAPPY AND GRATEFUL THAT I AM ENOUGH."

♥♥♥

NOW WRITE HOW YOU FEEL AFTER COMPLETING THIS EXCERCISE. DOES IT BRING ANYTHING UP FOR YOU? HOW DO YOU WANT TO FEEL TODAY?

....

....

....

Day 100!

SAY THIS AFFIRMATION OUT LOUD WITH YOUR HAND ON YOUR HEART:

NOW WRITE IT OUT 10 TIMES:

1 ....

....

2 ....

....

3 ....

....

4 ....

....

5 ....

....

6 ....

....

7 ....

....

8 ....

....

9 ....

....

10 ....

....

NOW REPEAT THIS THREE TIMES WITH YOUR HAND ON YOUR HEART:

♥♥♥

"I'M SO HAPPY AND GRATEFUL THAT I GET
TO LOVE MYSELF EVERY DAY."

♥♥♥

NOW WRITE HOW YOU FEEL AFTER COMPLETING THIS EXCERCISE. DOES IT BRING ANYTHING UP FOR YOU? HOW DO YOU WANT TO FEEL TODAY?

....

....

....

CONGRATULATIONS! LET'S SAY A LITTLE
SELF-LOVE MANTRA...

I am enough.
I've always been
enough.
I will always be
enough.

Belief-Busting

When practicing the affirmations, you may find some that don't feel very true at all and you may even feel some discomfort when writing and reading them out loud.

Pay close attention to these affirmations! It is likely that you have some deep, buried belief surrounding an issue and it's being highlighted for you. For example, if you found using the affirmation 'I am enough' uncomfortable or untrue, you may have some beliefs hidden in your subconscious about not being good enough or loveable because of something that was maybe said to you by a parent, schoolteacher, childhood friend or boss.

Be thankful for uncovering these old beliefs....and work to get rid of them! Use the next few pages to:
* Ask yourself where the belief started. Was it from an event or something that somebody said to you. Or maybe it was just what your parents believed so you subconsciously decided to try and fit in with them when you were younger.
* Ask yourself, is it true? Or was it someone's opinion? Was it passed on to you because of the way they were brought up? Is there any evidence that the opposite may also be true?
* Ask yourself whether this belief serves you in any way. Get really honest. Really honest! What are you gaining or holding on to by keeping this belief?
* If you could start to change that belief and find evidence of other people believing the new belief would you?
* If it's possible that this new belief could be true, start affirming this new belief to yourself. Out with the old, in with the new!

Belief:

Belief:

Belief:

Belief:

Belief:

Your Affirmations

Whilst working through the journal, you may very well be inspired to create your own affirmations. You may find that some just 'pop' into your head! Use this page to write them down so that you don't forget them. Sometimes you can think of an affirmation that might be more relevant, or maybe you are not ready for a big affirmation so your mind thinks of an easier one to act as a 'stepping stone'.

★ ....

....

....

....

....

★ ....

....

....

....

....

★ ....

....

....

....

....

★ ....
....
....
....
....

★ ....
....
....
....
....

★ ....
....
....
....
....

★ ....
....
....
....
....

Little Love Moments!

Everytime you feel confident or feel more love for yourself, write it down here. Perhaps when someone gives you a compliment or you manage to accomplish something big or small that you never thought you would be able to do before. When you feel proud of yourself, write it down. When you feel content with the way you are, write it down. When you handle a situation perfectly, write it down. When you recieve love and kindness from others, write it down. When you do something good for yourself, write it down.

This is a really powerful exercise to help you cement in the affirmations because you start to see and document the evidence that the new beliefs and affirmations are coming true. Use these pages to write them ALL down!

Little Love Moment:

Date:

Description:

Little Love Moment:

Date:
Description:

Little Love Moment:

Date:
Description:

Little Love Moment:

Date:
Description:

Little Love Moment:

Date:
Description:

Little Love Moment:

Date:
Description:

Little Love Moment:

Date:
Description:

Little Love Moment:

Date:
Description:

Little Love Moment:

Date:
Description:

Little Love Moment:

Date:
Description:

Little Love Moment:

Date:
Description:

Little Love Moment:

Date:
Description:

Little Love Moment:

Date:
Description:

Little Love Moment:

Date:
Description:

Little Love Moment:

Date:
Description:

Little Love Moment:

Date:
Description:

Little Love Moment:

Date:
Description:

Little Love Moment:

Date:
Description:

Little Love Moment:

Date:
Description:

Little Love Moment:

Date:
Description:

Little Love Moment:

Date:
Description:

Thank you x

IF YOU HAVE ENJOYED USING THIS BOOK PLEASE SPREAD THE LOVE WITH YOUR FAMILY, FRIENDS, WORK COLLEAGUES, AND COMMUNITY.

IF YOU PURCHASED THIS BOOK ON AMAZON AND WOULD LIKE TO REVIEW IT, WE WOULD BE ETERNALLY GRATEFUL!

PLEASE SIGN UP TO MY NEWSLETTER AT WWW.NATALIELOUISEFOX.COM

LOVE AND BLESSINGS ....

More Titles By Natalie L Fox:

Affirmations Journal For Wealth

ISBN: 978-0-9935382-1-6

Affirmations Journal For Health and Fitness

ISBN: 978-0-9935382-3-0

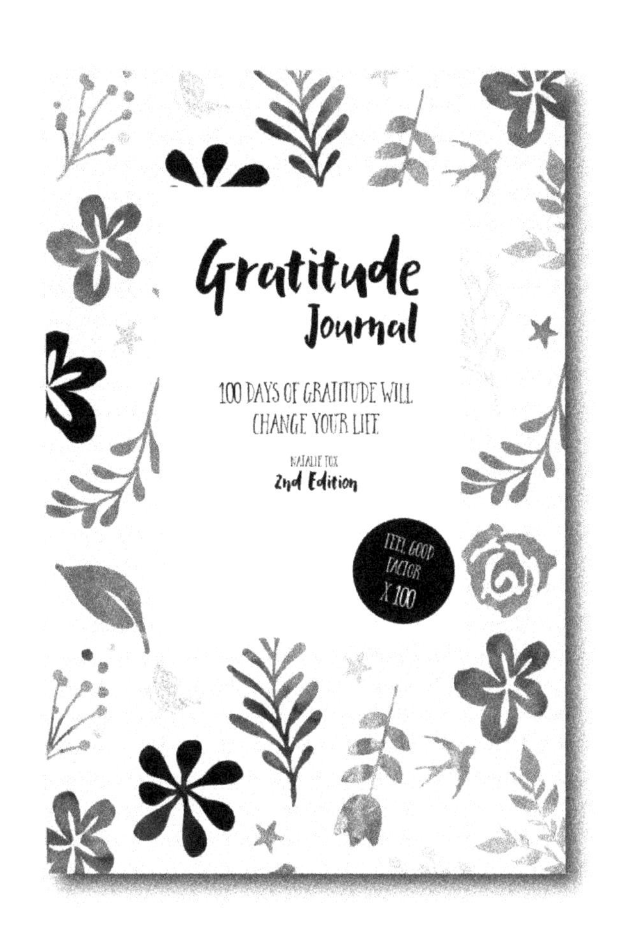

Gratitude Journal: 100 Days of Gratitude Will Change Your Life.
ISBN: 978-0-9935382-0-9

As seen in the Huffington Post

Lightning Source UK Ltd.
Milton Keynes UK
UKHW02f0041240518
323118UK00005B/148/P